Artificially-colored image of the Lagoon Nebula, a region of recently formed stars ab... ...h.

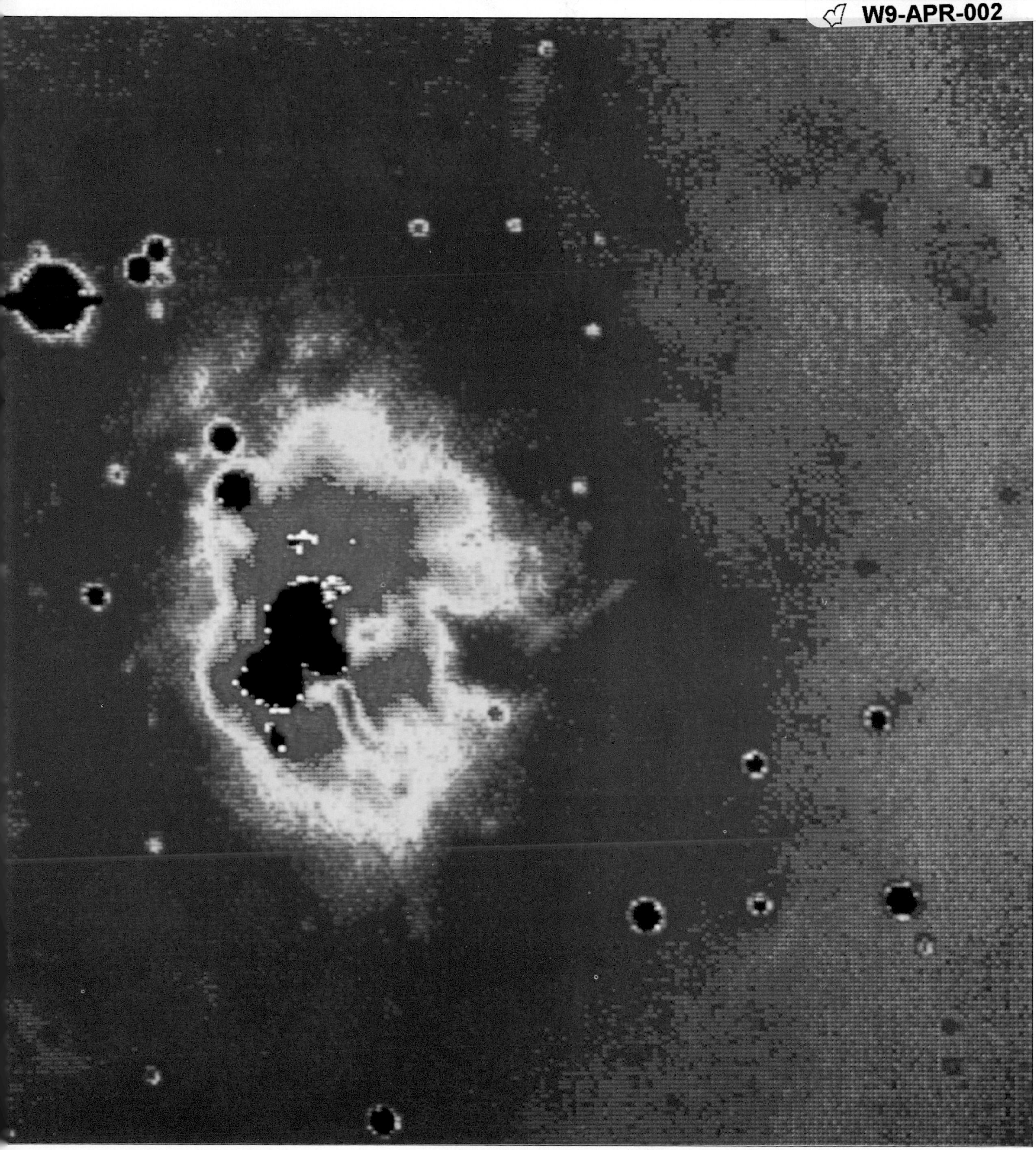

SPACE

The Trifid Nebula, a cloud of gas and dust situated about
3,000 light-years from us in the constellation of Sagittarius.

SCIENCE FACTS

SPACE

PETER LAFFERTY

Saturn and four of its moons as imaged by the Voyager 1 space probe in November 1980. The colors of the picture have been computer-enhanced.

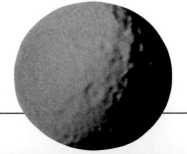

CRESCENT BOOKS
NEW YORK • AVENEL, NEW JERSEY

CLB 2834

© 1992 Colour Library Books Ltd., Godalming, Surrey, England.

This 1992 edition published by Crescent Books,
distributed by Outlet Book Company, Inc.,
a Random House Company
40 Engelhard Avenue, Avenel, New Jersey 07001

Printed and bound in Italy

ISBN 0 517 06555 X

8 7 6 5 4 3 2 1

The Author
Peter Lafferty is a fulltime author who specializes in science writing,
particularly with a younger audience in mind. His particular areas of interest
are astronomy, physics and chemistry, technology, computing, and the history
of science. He has written more than 35 books and has contributed to many
major encyclopedias.

Credits
Editor: Philip de Ste. Croix
Designer: Stonecastle Graphics Ltd.
Color artwork: Rod Ferring and Peter Bull © Colour Library Books Ltd.
Star maps: Paul Doherty
Picture Editor: Miriam Sharland
Production: Ruth Arthur, Sally Connolly, Neil Randles, Andrew Whitelaw
Director of Production: Gerald Hughes
Typesetting: SX Composing Ltd.
Color separations: Scantrans PTE Ltd, Singapore
Printed and bound by New Interlitho SpA, Italy

The colors in this picture of the
Sun have been treated to show
up sunspots and active regions
(yellow) and associated
filaments (blue).

CONTENTS

The sky at night

On a clear night go outside, away from the street lights, and look up at the starry sky. You will see a beautiful sight: thousands of stars scattered across the blackness of space. Across the sky, you will see a broad band of stars called the Milky Way. These stars are all relatively close to us. Like the Sun, they belong to a group of stars called the Milky Way Galaxy. A galaxy is a group of as many as 100,000 million stars – perhaps even more – collected together like a lit-up city in the vastness of space.

If your eyes are sharp, perhaps you will glimpse distant galaxies – dim indistinct objects that you cannot clearly make out. You might also see a faint nebula, a distant giant cloud of glowing gas in the space between the stars. Perhaps you will see a

The sky at twilight. When looking at the stars, you are looking backward in time. Light from the stars has taken many years, perhaps millions of years, to reach the Earth. So you are, in fact, seeing the stars as they were long ago.

The Sun is a star, the nearest to Earth. In many ways, the Sun is quite ordinary, but it is the only star known to have a family of planets circling around it. Its outpouring of energy, mainly in the form of light and heat, makes life possible on Earth.

Star trails and trees lit by a campfire. The colors of the different tracks are caused by the different types of stars making them, ranging from young, hot white stars to old and relatively cool orange and red stars.

An artificially-colored image of a spiral galaxy, containing about 100,000 million stars. It is 160 million million million miles (257 million million million km) away.

The ancient Greeks thought that the multitude of stars were fixed in a transparent dome of crystal material. This old picture shows a person looking through the dome into space.

'falling star,' a flash of light lancing silently through the dark sky. Or perhaps you will be intrigued by a bright object that does not seem to twinkle like the stars. This is a planet, one of the Sun's family.

Many people have looked at the stars as you are doing. Thousands of years ago when the first people walked the Earth, our ancestors looked up as you do. Their feelings may not have been much different from yours, for although we have a much better understanding of the Universe – space and everything in it – and the forces that work it, there are still many mysteries in the cosmos.

Perhaps the biggest mystery is that we can understand the Universe at all. After all, the Universe is so incredibly large and ancient. Here we are, sitting on a small planet moving around an average sort of star in an ordinary galaxy. Yet, thanks to modern science, we can reach out to the remote corners of the Universe – thousands of millions of miles or kilometers away – and understand much of what goes on there, in the depths of space.

Star stories

Our ancestors attempted to make sense of the world, just as we do. But, unlike us, they had very little information to go on. There was no accumulated 'data bank' of facts, built up by careful observation over the centuries. So they could not see that there are patterns and regularities in the natural world, patterns that can be used to explain the workings of Nature in a systematic way. To them the world must have seemed a mysterious, capricious, and random place.

The explanation of Nature's mysteries put forward by all early people was that there were powerful beings called gods who worked the world much as a puppeteer works the strings of a puppet. Mostly these gods were invisible and unseen but occasionally they ventured to walk the Earth. The stories of their adventures explained why the winds blew and the rains fell, why the Sun rose and set each day, and why the stars appeared to make patterns in the sky. For example, to the ancient Aztecs of Mexico, the Sun was a god, Huitzilopochtli, who died each night, and needed human blood in order to rise again each morning. Each year 15,000 men were sacrificed to the sun-god.

Traces of the gods were most clearly seen in the night sky. The star patterns, which we call constellations, were thought to be outlines of the gods or their companions. For instance, the constellation of Orion, the great hunter, dominates the winter skies in northern countries. Some

The stars Merak and Dubhe are called 'the pointers' because a line drawn through them points to the Pole Star, Polaris, which always lies to the north. A line through Mizar and Polaris points to Cassiopeia.

The constellation of Orion, the Hunter. Orion dominates the southern winter skies for northern stargazers. In the southern hemisphere, it is a northern constellation of the summer skies. The three stars forming Orion's belt are seen in the center.

Part of the constellation of Ursa Major called the Big Dipper or the Plough. In the center of the image is Phad, with Dubhe and Merak toward the lower right. The three bright stars forming the 'handle' are Alioth, Mizar, and Alkaid.

A 1493 engraving showing how the Egyptian astronomer Ptolemy (about A.D. 100-170) thought the Sun and planets revolved around the Earth (center) on concentric spheres. Outside the planetary spheres, God and nine classes of angel preside.

The constellation of Gemini, the Heavenly Twins. The twins are the stars Castor and Pollux, seen by the faces of the two figures – Castor at the right and Pollux at the left. In Greek mythology, they were the sons of Leda and Zeus, the ruler of the gods.

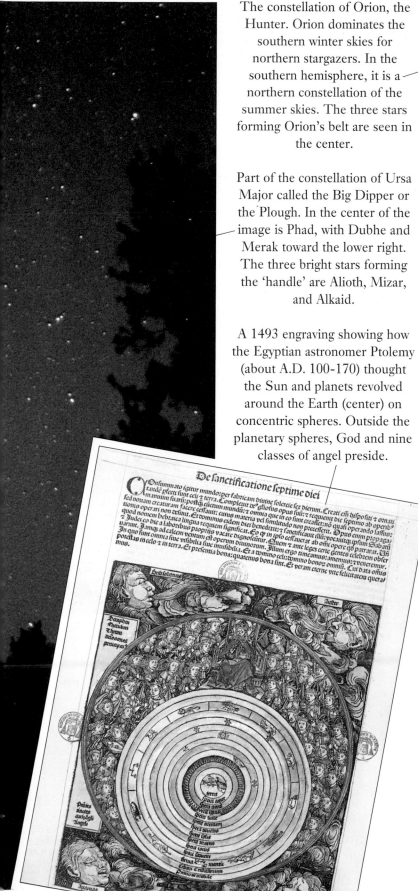

distance from Orion's foot is a constellation outlining the Scorpion who, so legend relates, stung Orion and killed him.

Various systems of identifying constellations have been used over the ages. The Egyptians recognized one set of constellations, the Chinese another. The system we use today comes mainly from the Greeks. It identifies 88 constellations in all, covering the entire sky. Each constellation has a story to tell. The Great Bear who walks through the northern sky was once a beautiful princess who was placed in the sky because Juno the queen of gods became jealous. The Greek hero Perseus can be seen side by side with King Cepheus and his queen Cassiopeia. Individual stars also have names and stories attached to them. These stories transform the night sky into a giant storybook.

Star science

Scientists use careful observation, experiments, and apply ideas or theories to study the Universe. Astronomy – the science that studies the planets, stars, galaxies, and other objects found in outer space – is especially difficult. Planets, stars, and galaxies are far away from the Earth. How can astronomers study such distant objects?

Luckily, we receive messages from the stars and galaxies. These messages are carried by the light and other radiation that the stars and galaxies are pouring outward into space. Astronomers use giant telescopes to catch the light, and a variety of instruments to decode the messages of the stars. For instance, the chemical composition of a star can be found by examining the starlight with an instrument called a spectroscope which splits light into its constituent colors.

But light is not the only messenger from the stars and galaxies. Radio waves, ultraviolet rays, heat or infrared rays, powerful X-rays called gamma rays, all stream down on the Earth from space. Special telescopes have been developed to study these rays. Also, many tiny particles of matter called cosmic rays reach us from space. These particles are produced when the atoms of gas found in space are broken up by the violent events occurring in the Universe.

The experiments of Earth-bound scientists reveal the forces of Nature: gravity, electric and magnetic forces, and the hidden forces that hold together the center part or nucleus of an atom. The greatest discovery of astronomy is that these forces act in all corners of the Universe, not just on Earth.

By using the latest ideas or theories about these forces, we can in our imagination explore the far reaches of space. We can understand why stars come together to form galaxies when we realize that the force of gravity acts upon all objects in

A scientist using an infrared dectector to 'see' the beam of an infrared laser. The laser is part of an ultra-accurate atomic clock.

space. We can understand how the stars generate their enormous outpourings of light and energy by taking account of the nuclear forces acting inside the atoms that make up the stars. Thus, in the end, the brains of scientists turn out to be the most powerful tools for exploring the Universe.

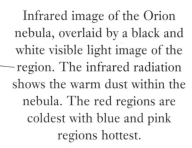

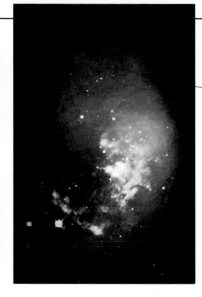

Infrared image of the Orion nebula, overlaid by a black and white visible light image of the region. The infrared radiation shows the warm dust within the nebula. The red regions are coldest with blue and pink regions hottest.

X-ray contour map of the Orion nebula, overlaid with a visible light photograph of the region. Newly-formed stars show up prominently as bright X-ray sources.

The Orion nebula, photographed using visible light. The nebula is a great cloud of dust containing many young stars. The nebula is found in Orion's sword and can be seen with the unaided eye.

Artificially-colored radio image of the Orion nebula, showing radio emission from carbon monoxide gas. The most intense radiation is colored black, below this come red, yellow, and blue, and the faintest emission is shown pink.

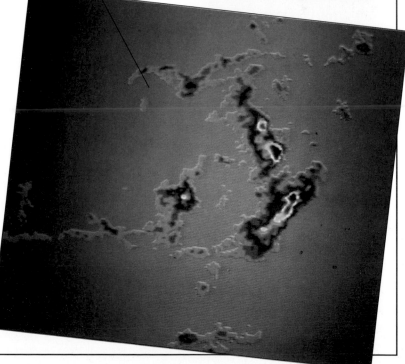

Photograph of an evening primrose flower taken using daylight. It seems uniform in color to us, but there are 'honey guides' visible to insects.

Evening primrose photographed using ultraviolet light. The UV radiation reveals the 'honey guides' (dark areas), invisible in ordinary light.

With the naked eye – before the telescope

Astronomy is an ancient science. It seems likely that Stonehenge in Southern England was built about 4,000 years ago as an astronomical observatory. The Great Pyramid at Cheops, Egypt, was built by the ancient Egyptians about 2,550 B.C. As well as being a tomb, the pyramid was used as an observatory. One of the earliest astronomical discoveries was that although most stars had fixed positions relative to each other, there were objects that moved amongst the stars. These wanderers were called planets (from the Greek word meaning wanderer). In ancient times, five planets were known: Mercury, Venus, Mars, Jupiter, and Saturn. The paths of the planets among the stars puzzled early astronomers. A great Greek astronomer called Ptolemy who lived in Alexandria in Egypt in the second century A.D. had an explanation of the planets' motions. According to Ptolemy, the planets were moving in circles around the Earth. The Sun and Moon were also thought to circle around the Earth. In 1576 Danish astronomer Tycho Brahe made very accurate measurements of the movements of the planets, particularly Mars. Brahe discovered that Ptolemy's theory could not explain his measurements of Mars' path so he proposed an alternative theory. According to Brahe, the planets moved around the Sun, and the Sun moved around the Earth. Although this was a step in the right direction, Brahe could not bring himself to believe that the Earth itself was moving.

In this 1508 engraving, the ancient astronomer Ptolemy measures the position of a star using an instrument called a quadrant.

Danish astronomer Tycho Brahe's observatory where he made the most accurate measurements of stars possible with the naked eye.

Tycho Brahe in his observatory on the island of Hveen, between Sweden and Denmark. Brahe used a giant quadrant to observe the stars and the planets.

The planet Mars (center) in the constellation of Taurus. The bright star below Mars is Aldebaran. The Pleiades cluster is at the upper right.

The Moon blocks out the Sun during an eclipse at Stonehenge, in England. The alignments of the stones may have been used to make astronomical predictions.

❏ The great Danish astronomer Tycho Brahe (1546-1601) was known as 'the astronomer with the golden nose.' He had part of his nose sliced off in a duel, and made himself a replacement from gold, silver, and wax.

❏ Within each consellation, stars are labelled using the letters of the Greek alphabet: alpha, beta, gamma, and so on down to the last letter of the alphabet, omega. The brightest star is called alpha, the second brightest is called beta, and so on. For example, the brightest star in the constellation of Cygnus, the Swan, is called Alpha Cygni.

❏ Stars often have Arabic names, harking back to the great days of Arab astronomy in the ninth and tenth centuries during which a famous school of astronomy flourished in Baghdad. For instance, Alpha Orionis, a bright star in the Orion constellation, is also called Betelgeuse. This is the Arab word for 'shoulder;' the star indicates where the Great Hunter's shoulder is in the pattern of this constellation.

❏ The star with the longest name in astronomy is 'Shurnarkabtishashutu' which is Arabic for 'under the southern horn of the bull.'

❏ There are around 6,000 stars visible to the naked eye although an Earthbound observer can only see half the sky at one time.

The telescope – window on the universe

Italian astronomer Galileo Galilei (1564-1642) who first applied the telescope to astronomy.

In 1608, in the Dutch town of Middelburg, spectacle maker Hans Lippershey made an important discovery. While idly toying with some spectacle lenses, he noticed that a distant weather vane looked ncarcr and larger when viewed through two lenses. Being a practical person, Lippershey soon constructed a long tube to hold the lenses in place. So, the telescope was born. News of the invention soon spread. In Italy, the famous scientist Galileo Galilei made a telescope that magnified objects by nine times. When he turned his telescope to the night sky, Galileo saw that the Moon had mountains and round craters. He saw that the Milky Way contained millions of stars never before seen. He discovered that the planet Jupiter had four moons circling around it. The problem with lens telescopes (called refracting telescopes, or refractors) was that they had to be very long to produce a sharp image. In addition, bright objects seen through these telescopes often seemed to have bright colored edges. The colors were caused because white light is a mixture of all colors of the rainbow. The colors are revealed when light passes through the lens. In 1668, English scientist Isaac Newton solved these problems by building a telescope that used a mirror instead of lenses to collect the light. Newton's telescope was much shorter than a lens telescope and did not produce colored edges. Since then, almost all large telescopes have used mirrors. Telescopes that use mirrors are called reflectors.

A model of Isaac Newton's telescope, the first such instrument to use a mirror to collect light. Mirror telescopes, called reflectors, had several advantages over the lens telescopes used previously. Today reflecting telescopes are the main instruments of astronomers.

The common frog has large eyes to collect light efficiently, allowing the animal to see in the dark. The efficiency of a telescope also depends upon the amount of light collected, and so the larger the better.

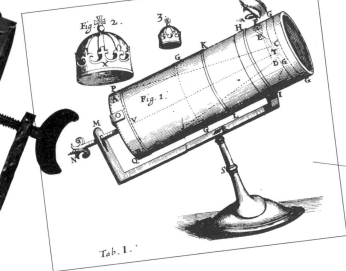

Isaac Newton's design for his reflecting telescope. It was 6in (15cm) long by 1in (2.5cm) in diameter, and could magnify about 30 times.

Types of telescopes. The Galilean telescope uses a large convex lens (called the objective) at the front and a concave lens as the eyepiece. The Newtonian telescope uses a small mirror to direct light from the main mirror into the eyepiece. The terrestrial telescope has an additional lens between the objective and the eyepiece. This extra lens ensures that the image seen is not inverted, but is the correct way up.

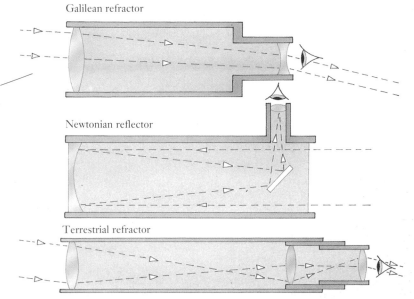

Galilean refractor

Newtonian reflector

Terrestrial refractor

❏ The Old Royal Observatory at Greenwich, London, was founded by Charles II in 1675. He paid for the building work by selling old and decayed gunpowder to the French. The observatory was set up to find a way of navigating at sea using the stars. A young astronomer, John Flamsteed, was appointed as 'Astronomer Royal' to make the necessary observations of the stars and planets, at a salary of £100 a year. He stayed in the job for 45 years.

❏ The 'Leviathan of Parsonstown' was a huge 72in (183cm) telescope built in 1845 by the Third Earl of Rosse, William Parsons. It was so large that it could not be moved to point at particular stars; astronomers had to wait until the turning of the Earth carried a star through the telescope's field of view.

❏ The largest telescope lens ever made was 59in (150cm) across. It was shown in a Paris exhibition in 1900. Unfortunately, the giant lens was flawed and was never used for scientific work.

❏ James Lick, who made millions by property speculation in San Francisco, paid for an observatory to be built in 1868 on top of Mount Hamilton in Northern California. When he died in 1876, Lick was buried beneath one of the telescopes, the world's second largest lens telescope.

Today's telescopes

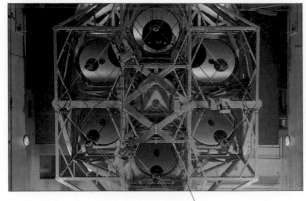

In a mirror telescope, the mirror acts like a giant eye, collecting light from a faint and distant star. The captured light is focused on to an eyepiece, photographic plate, or an electronic light detector. The larger the mirror, the more light that is collected and the fainter the stars that can be seen. For this reason, astronomers have always hankered after larger and larger telescopes. Today, the world's largest single-mirror telescope is in the Caucasus Mountains, Russia. Its mirror weighs 77 tons (70 tonnes) and is 236in (6m) across. The telescope is so sensitive that it can detect a single candle 15,000 miles (24,000km) away. The next largest telescope is the Hale telescope at Mount Palomar, near Pasadena, California. This has a mirror 200in (508cm) across that weighs 22 tons (20 tonnes). But there is a limit to the size of a mirror. If the mirror is too large, it bends under its own weight and cannot produce a clear image. So, instead of using a single very large mirror, the latest telescopes combine the light collected by several smaller mirrors. The Multiple Mirror Telescope at Mount Hopkins, Arizona, uses six 72in (183cm) mirrors combined. The combined mirrors are equivalent to a large single mirror 176in (447cm) across. Other telescopes are being built that take the idea further. For example, the Keck telescope being built in Mauna Kea, Hawaii, will have a mirror 393in (1,000cm) across, made up of 36 segments fitted together. The relative positions of each mirror segment have to be controlled to within one thousandth of the breadth of a human hair.

The Multiple Mirror Telescope on Mount Hopkins, Arizona. It consists of six separate mirrors, each 72in (183cm) in diameter. Since it began operating in 1979, the MMT has proved the feasibility of using a number of small mirrors to provide the light-grasp of a single giant mirror.

The 200in (508cm) Hale telescope in its dome at Mount Palomar, California. The 'transparent dome' effect was created by rotating the dome with its shutter open during a long exposure photograph.

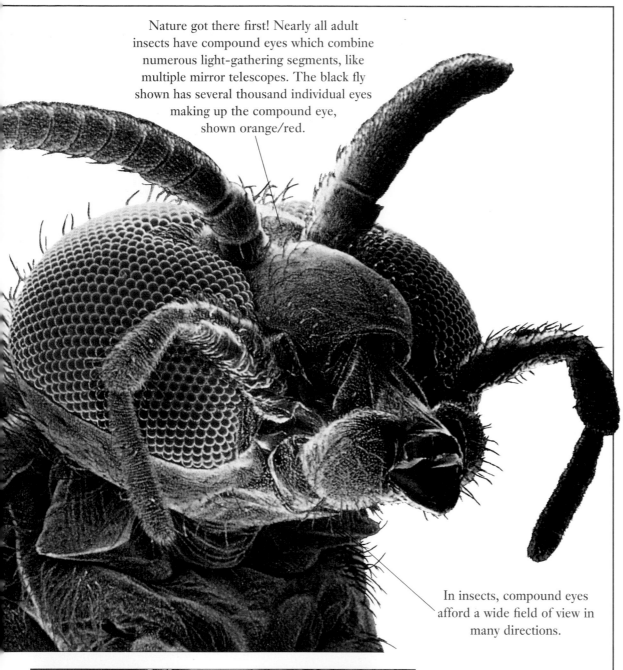

Nature got there first! Nearly all adult insects have compound eyes which combine numerous light-gathering segments, like multiple mirror telescopes. The black fly shown has several thousand individual eyes making up the compound eye, shown orange/red.

In insects, compound eyes afford a wide field of view in many directions.

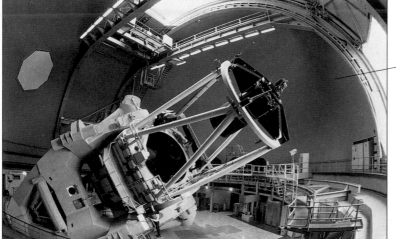

The 12.5ft (381cm) telescope at the European Southern Observatory site at La Silla, Chile. Modern astronomers rarely look through their telescopes optically. For years most observations have been recorded on photographic plates and, more recently, by electronic sensors called charge-coupled devices, or as computer data to be analyzed later. The computer screen provides a visual picture.

FACT FILE

TOP TELESCOPES

❑ Keck Telescope, Mauna Kea, Hawaii, 36 hexagonal mirror segments each 71in (180cm) across, fitted together to make a mirror almost 33ft (1,000cm) across when completed.

❑ Mount Semirodriki, Caucasus, Russia, built 1976, single mirror 236in (600cm) across. Largest single mirror telescope, but has not performed up to expectations.

❑ Hale Telescope, Mount Palomar, near Pasadena, California, built 1948, single mirror 200in (508cm) across.

❑ William Herschel Telescope, La Palma, Canary Islands, built 1987, single mirror 165in (420cm) across.

❑ Anglo-Australian Telescope, Siding Springs, Australia, built 1974, single mirror 153in (389cm) across.

❑ New Technology Telescope, La Silla, Chile, 12.5ft (381cm), computer-controlled flexible mirror system which adjusts the shape of the mirror 100 times a second to achieve better viewing.

❑ UKIT, United Kingdom Infrared Telescope, Mauna Kea, Hawaii, single mirror 147in (374cm) across. The performance is so good that it is also used for observing with visible light as well as infrared.

Radio telescopes

The 330ft (100m) diameter dish of the Effelsberg radio telescope near Bonn, Germany. The telescope, weighing 3,350 tons (3,048 tonnes), is the world's largest fully-steerable, single dish radio telescope. The outer part of the dish is made from mesh to prevent the wind distorting its shape.

In 1931 American engineer Karl Jansky accidentally picked up radio waves from space using an antenna from a car radio. This was the beginning of radio astronomy. Radio telescopes detect radio waves that come from distant stars and galaxies. The waves are collected in a large dish and focused on to the antenna of a sensitive radio receiver. The electrical signal produced by the receiver is usually fed to a computer display screen that shows a picture of the sky seen through radio 'eyes.'

Because radio waves are longer than light waves, radio telescopes have to be larger than optical telescopes to produce the same seeing power. The world's largest radio telescope, at Arecibo, Puerto Rico, is over 1,000ft (305m) across. Its dish was hollowed out of a valley in the mountains. It can pick up signals a million million times weaker than a small light bulb. However, there is a limit to the size of telescope that can be built. So astronomers link together two or more radio telescopes in order to improve the performance. If two small dishes of 42ft (13m) diameter spaced 0.62 miles (1km) apart are linked, the effectiveness of the combined system is 70 times greater than that of the individual instruments. A large system of dishes known as the Very Large Array has been built at Socorro, New Mexico. It consists of 27 mobile radio telescopes on a Y-shaped railway track. The system is equivalent to a single dish 21 miles (34km) across.

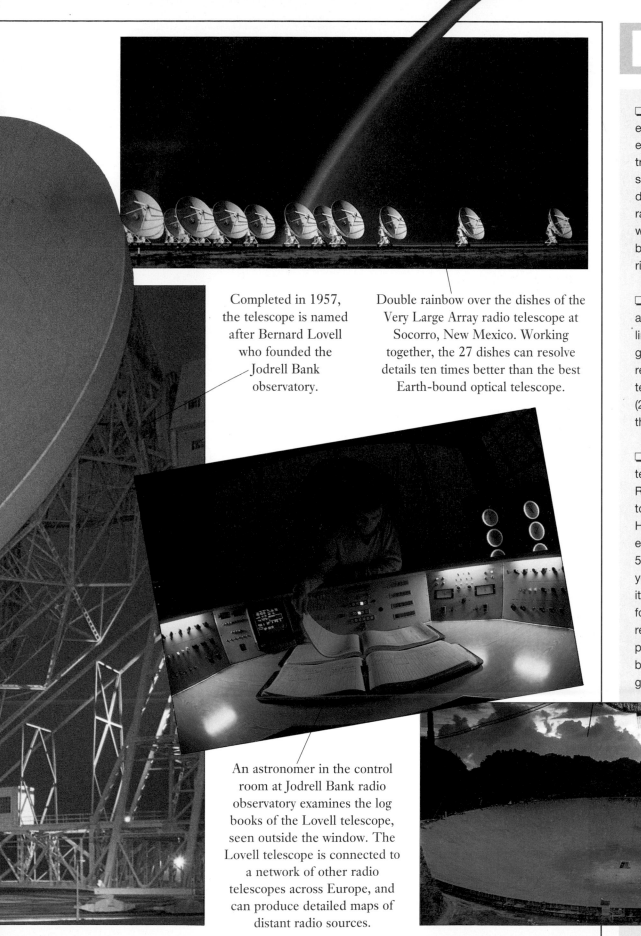

Completed in 1957, the telescope is named after Bernard Lovell who founded the Jodrell Bank observatory.

Double rainbow over the dishes of the Very Large Array radio telescope at Socorro, New Mexico. Working together, the 27 dishes can resolve details ten times better than the best Earth-bound optical telescope.

❏ Radio waves are ripples of electricity and magnetism – electromagnetic waves – that travel through space at the speed of light. The only difference between light and radio waves lies in their wavelength, the distance between successive wave ripples.

❏ Radio telescopes in orbit around the Earth have been linked with telescopes on the ground to form a system with a resolution equivalent to a radio telescope 17,000 miles (25,500km) across, over twice the diameter of the Earth.

❏ In 1974 the giant radio telescope at Arecibo, Puerto Rico, beamed a message toward a cluster of stars. However, an answer cannot be expected until around the year 50,000. It will take 25,000 years for the message to reach its target, and the same time for any answer transmitted to reach us back on Earth. The picture below shows dawn breaking over the telescope's giant radio dish.

An astronomer in the control room at Jodrell Bank radio observatory examines the log books of the Lovell telescope, seen outside the window. The Lovell telescope is connected to a network of other radio telescopes across Europe, and can produce detailed maps of distant radio sources.

Searching high and low

Not all telescopes are to be found in mountain-top observatories. One important telescope is 4,850ft (1.5km) underground in the Homestake Mine, South Dakota. The 'telescope' consists of a large tank of dry cleaning fluid, as tall as a four-story building. This is a neutrino telescope. It detects tiny bits of matter called neutrinos given out by the Sun and other stars. When a neutrino passes through the tank, some of the atoms in the liquid become radioactive. So, the sudden appearance of radioactive atoms in the tank shows that neutrinos have passed through. At the other extreme, high above the Earth, telescopes are found in orbit. The most famous orbiting telescope is the Hubble Space Telescope, named after a well-known American astronomer, Edwin Hubble. The Hubble Space Telescope was launched from Kennedy Space Center aboard a Space Shuttle in April 1990. Unfortunately, the telescope is not yet performing as it should, because of an error made during the manufacture of the mirror. Scientists hope to correct the error by undertaking a repair mission at a future date. There have been many other orbiting telescopes and observatories launched into space. These provide a window on the Universe that is closed to Earth-bound astronomers. This is because the Earth's atmosphere absorbs many types of radiation, such as ultraviolet radiation and X-rays, for example, and so observations of these rays cannot be carried out on the ground. Instead, satellites are used. For instance, the International Ultraviolet Explorer, launched in 1978, provided valuable data for a decade. The Einstein X-ray Observatory, also launched in 1978, discovered that almost all stars emit X-rays.

The Einstein X-ray Observatory during pre-flight checking. Standing 19ft (5.8m) high, the satellite was launched in 1978. During a 2½-year life, it revolutionized X-ray astronomy.

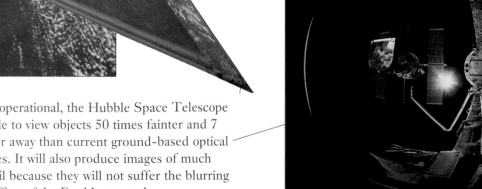

Deployment of the Hubble Space Telescope from the Space Shuttle *Discovery* on April 24, 1990. The telescope is still attached to the Shuttle by the remote manipulator arm (bottom) and is unfurling the first of its solar panels (foreground). At the left is one of the two dish antennae.

The giant tank of dry-cleaning fluid which forms the neutrino detector at the Homestake Mine, South Dakota. Neutrinos coming from the Sun and stars interact with the fluid to produce radioactive argon. The detector is situated deep underground.

When fully operational, the Hubble Space Telescope will be able to view objects 50 times fainter and 7 times further away than current ground-based optical telescopes. It will also produce images of much greater detail because they will not suffer the blurring effect of the Earth's atmosphere.

❑ A satellite uses only a small amount of electricity, about the same as two household light bulbs.

❑ The Hubble Space Telescope, the space-based telescope launched from Shuttle *Discovery* in April 1990, has a 94.5in (240cm) mirror. It is powerful enough to see a small coin 450 miles (724km) away. This is the distance between New York and Detroit. It can detect light from a two-cell flashlight over 250,000 miles (400,000km) away.

❑ The Einstein X-ray Observatory has been lost. After 2½ years successful operation, contact with the satellite was lost in 1981. Presumably, it is still in orbit above the Earth at a height of about 500 miles (800km).

❑ Neutrinos pass easily through solid material at the speed of light. A neutrino could pass through a solid piece of lead 600 million million miles (965 million million km) thick without being absorbed. Millions of neutrinos will pass through you while you read this sentence.

❑ NASA's Gamma Ray Observatory, launched in 1991, picks up the most powerful type of radiation – gamma rays. The 15.9 ton (14 tonne) GRO orbits at a height of 280 miles (450km), mapping the very edges of the Universe.

The Sun's family

The main members of the Sun's family – the Solar System – are the nine planets that move around it in almost circular orbits: Mercury, Venus, Earth, Mars, Jupiter, Saturn, Uranus, Neptune, and Pluto. All the planets except Venus and Mercury have moons. There are at least 60 moons in the Solar System. In between the orbits of Mars and

Polish astronomer Nicolaus Copernicus (1473-1543) who showed that the planets move around the Sun.

Jupiter, there are many millions of small rocky bodies called asteroids. Finally, there are 100 billion comets orbiting the Sun in elongated oval-shaped orbits. It is difficult to grasp the size of the Solar System. To help, try to imagine a model of it. If the Sun was the size of a beach ball 3ft (90cm) across, then Mercury would be the size of a peppercorn 123ft (37m) away. Venus would be the size of a pea, 231ft (70m) away. The Earth would be the size of a pea, 321ft (98m) away. Mars would be the size of a peppercorn, 489ft (149m) away. Jupiter would be an apple, 1,668ft (508m) away. Saturn would be a tangerine, 3,060ft (933m) away. Uranus would be a table tennis ball, 1.1 miles (1.8km) away. Neptune would also be a table tennis ball, 1.8 miles (2.9km) away, and Pluto would be a pinhead, 2.4 miles (3.8km) from the Sun.

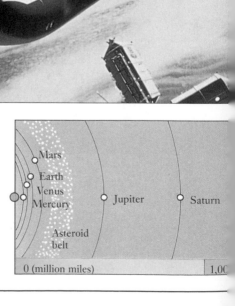

An artist's impression of the Earth and outer planets (closest first): Mars, the asteroids, Jupiter, Saturn, Uranus, and Neptune.

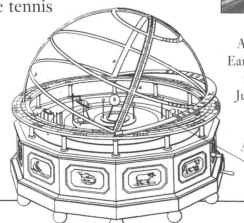

An orrery, a clockwork model used to show the motions of the planets.

Mars
Earth
Venus
Mercury
Jupiter
Saturn
Asteroid belt
0 (million miles)
1,00

❏ In the early 1500s, Polish astronomer Nicolaus Copernicus first established that the planets all move around the Sun, rather than the Sun and planets circling the Earth, as was previously believed. However, he was afraid to publish his ideas that went against established Church doctrine. A book describing his theory – *On the Revolution of the Celestial Spheres* – was printed in 1543, and a copy delivered to Copernicus as he lay on his deathbed.

❏ The most inaccurate estimate of the Sun's size was made in the sixth century B.C. by a Greek astronomer, Heraclitus. He decided that the Sun was 1ft (30cm) across; in fact, it is nearly 870,000 miles (1.4 million km) across.

❏ Apollo astronauts took 3 days to travel to the Moon. At these speeds, astronauts would take 11 months to reach Venus, 1 year 8 months to reach Mars, 2 years to reach Mercury, 13 years to reach Jupiter, 30 years to reach Saturn, 61 years to reach Uranus, 96 years to reach Neptune, and 126 years to reach Pluto.

❏ Light takes . . . 1.25 seconds to travel from the Moon to Earth, . . . 8 minutes 27 seconds to travel from the Sun to Earth, . . . 6 hours to travel from Pluto to Earth.

Average distances of the planets from the Sun. The orbits of the planets are ellipses, or slightly flattened circles. The deviation of the orbits from a circular shape is small however. Pluto is the only planet with an obviously elliptical orbit.

Uranus   Neptune   Pluto

2,000   3,000

The Moon – Earth's companion

The most expensive rocks of all time were the Moon rocks brought back to Earth by the Apollo astronauts in the late 1960s and early 1970s. In all, 12 men visited the Moon, starting with Neil Armstrong who stepped out on to the Moon on July 20, 1969. The last man on the Moon (so far!) was Eugene Cernan who visited the Moon in December 1972. The astronauts brought back to Earth 842lb (380kg) of Moon rocks and soil, taken from six different locations. Since the total cost of the Apollo program was $25 billion, the rocks and soil cost nearly $30 million per pound. The Apollo astronauts did much more than collect rocks – about 25 different experiments were completed. Instruments placed on the surface sent signals back to Earth for more than eight years after Cernan flew home, measuring moonquakes, meteorite impacts, magnetism, and heat flow. A mirror left on the surface was used to measure the distance to the Moon with unprecedented accuracy. On May 9, 1972, a laser fired from an observatory on Earth was reflected off the mirror by scientists at the Massachusetts Institute of Technology. By measuring the time taken for the light to travel to the mirror, and back, the distance to the Moon could be calculated. The result? The Moon is 233,813 miles (376,275km) from the Earth.

As the Moon circles the Earth, its appearance changes through a regular cycle of shapes called phases. The outer spheres on the diagram show the view of the Moon seen from Earth. The phases occur because different parts of the Moon are in shadow at different times.

Full Moon

Gibbous (waxing)

First quarter

Crescent

Sunlight

Earth

New Moon

Gibbous (waning)

Last quarter

Crescent

❏ The Moon is the sixth largest satellite in the Solar System. The larger satellites are: Jupiter's moons, Io, Ganymede, and Callisto; Saturn's Titan; and Neptune's Triton.

❏ The first spacecraft to send back pictures of the far side of the Moon was Luna 3 in October 1959. The photographs covered about 70 percent of the far side.

❏ The largest crater that can be seen on the Moon is called Bailly or the 'fields of ruin.' It covers an area of about 26,000 square miles (67,300km^2), about the size of West Virginia, and over three times the size of Wales.

❏ The temperature on the Moon reaches 243°F (117°C) at midday on the lunar equator. During the night, the temperature falls to −261°F (−162°C).

❏ The footprints left by the Apollo astronauts will not erode since there is no wind or water on the Moon. The footprints should last at least 10 million years.

❏ The brightest crater on the Moon is Aristarchus, named after ancient Greek astronomer Aristarchus of Samos (about 310-250 B.C.). The rocks of crater Aristarcus reflect twice as much light as the average moon rocks. It is 25 miles (40km) across and 10,000ft (3km) deep.

Using a powerful telescope, about 500,000 craters can be seen on the face of the Moon which is turned toward the Earth. If you started to count the craters at a rate of one each second, it would take nearly six days to complete the count.

This view from the Apollo 11 spacecraft shows the Earth rising above the Moon's horizon. The terrain pictured is an area known as Smyth's Sea.

Charles Duke, lunar module pilot of Apollo 16, collecting rock samples near the Descartes highlands landing site. The lunar roving vehicle is in the background.

Here shown drawn to the same scale as the U.S.A., the diameter of the Moon, 2,160 miles (3,476km), is one-quarter that of the Earth. The mass of the Earth is 81 times greater than that of the Moon.

The dynamic Sun

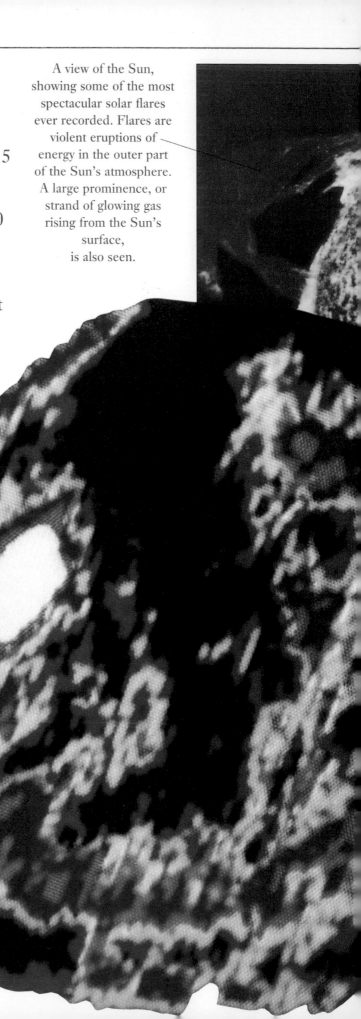

At the center of the Sun the temperature is 27 million °F (15 million °C). If a grain of sand was heated to this temperature, its heat would set alight everything within 60 miles (100km) of it. The Sun has a mean diameter of 865,000 miles (1,392,000km). This is 110 times the diameter of the Earth. In volume, the Sun is 1,300,000 times larger than the Earth. The mass of the Sun is about 2.2 billion billion billion tons (2 billion billion billion tonnes), about 333,420 times that of the Earth. The huge size and mass of the Sun means that the outer layers press inward with tremendous pressure – more than 200 billion times the Earth's atmospheric pressure. At these pressures and temperatures, the hydrogen making up the Sun ignites and the Sun becomes a huge nuclear bomb. Energy is released deep within the Sun by a process called nuclear fusion. During nuclear fusion, hydrogen nuclei – the center parts of hydrogen atoms – combine to form helium. This releases energy. The same process occurs inside a hydrogen bomb but, of course, on a much smaller scale. The Sun's outpouring of energy is equivalent to 100,000 million hydrogen bombs exploding each second.

A view of the Sun, showing some of the most spectacular solar flares ever recorded. Flares are violent eruptions of energy in the outer part of the Sun's atmosphere. A large prominence, or strand of glowing gas rising from the Sun's surface, is also seen.

Albert Einstein (1879-1955), a German-born American whose theories explain the energy source of the Sun. In his theory of relativity, Einstein showed that mass and energy are equivalent, and that matter can be converted into energy. This conversion process takes place in nuclear bombs, nuclear reactors, and inside the stars.

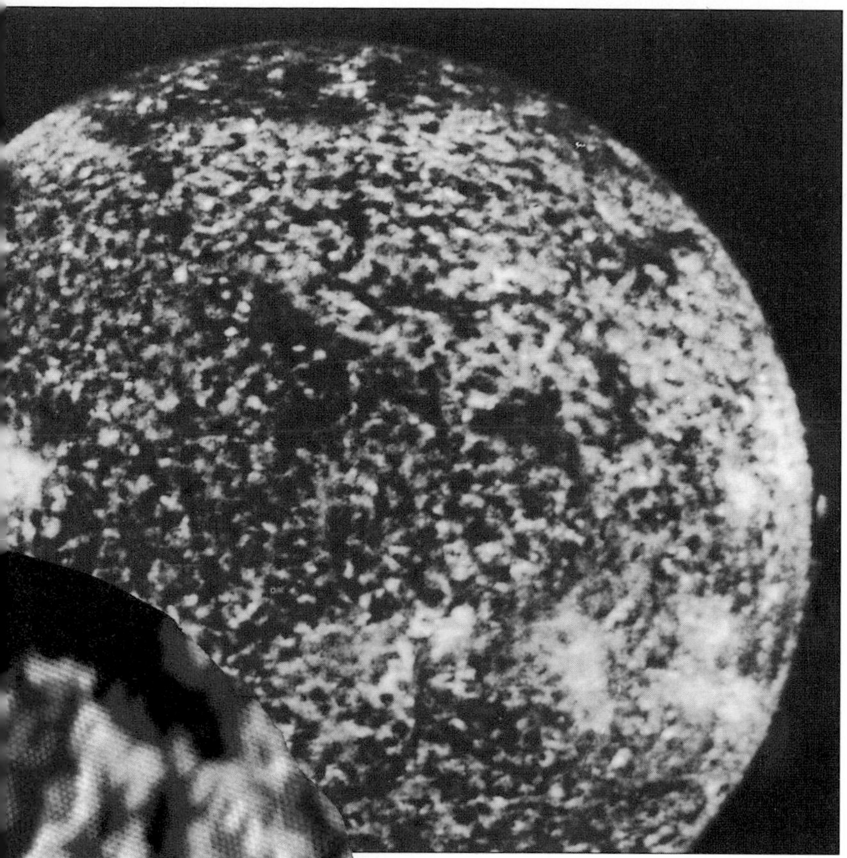

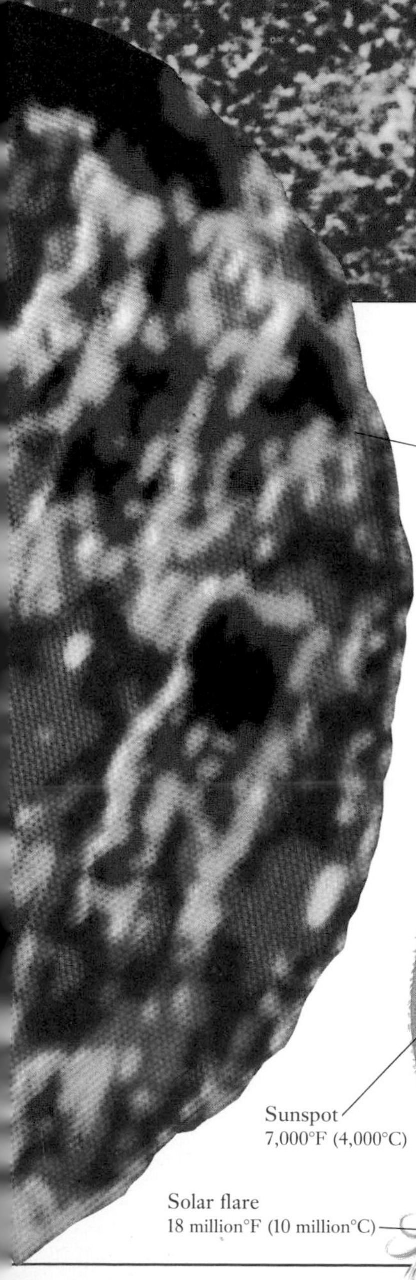

Laboratories around the world are trying to build a nuclear fusion reactor which would harness the Sun's energy source. Nuclear fusion power would be safe, clean, and cheap. The picture shows the electrical transformers used at the fusion laboratory at Culham, England.

An ultraviolet image of the Sun showing a boot-shaped hole (black area) in the corona, or upper part of the Sun's atmosphere. The hole allows an outflow of gas and electrically-charged particles called the solar wind to occur.

The visible surface layer of the Sun is called the photosphere. Above the photosphere lies the chromosphere and the corona. The Sun's energy is generated in the central core. The energy can take 10 million years to reach the surface from the center.

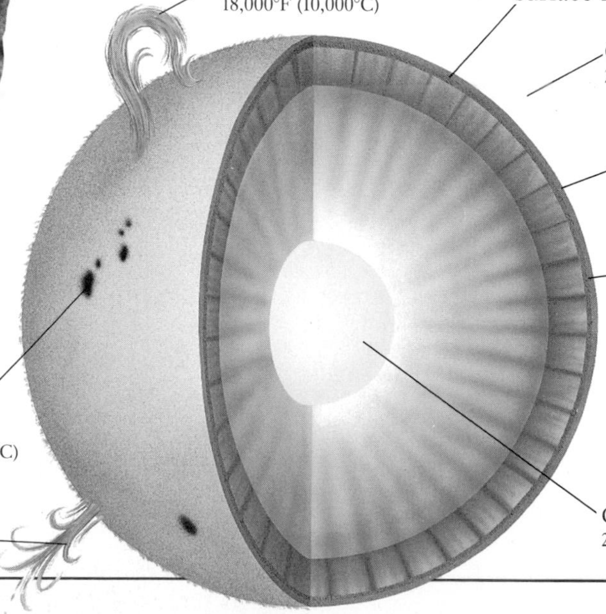

Prominence
18,000°F (10,000°C)

Corona
2,700,000°F (1,500,000°C)

Chromosphere
18,000°F (10,000°C)

Photosphere
11,000°F (6,000°C)

Sunspot
7,000°F (4,000°C)

Solar flare
18 million°F (10 million°C)

Core
27 million°F (15 million°C)

❏ The Sun converts 4.5 million tons (4 million tonnes) of mass to energy every second, equivalent to the weight of a million elephants each second. However, we need not worry about the Sun running out of fuel – at least, not just yet. It has enough fuel to burn for another 5,000 million years.

❏ The Sun's energy production each second is enough to supply the electrical needs of the U.S.A. for 50 million years.

❏ An area of the Sun's surface the size of a postage stamp (one square inch or 6.25cm^2) shines with the power of 1,500,000 candles.

❏ Giant flames called prominences shoot out from the Sun's surface for 310,000 miles (500,000km), more than the distance from the Earth to the Moon. The entire Earth could fit into one of these flames nearly 40 times.

❏ The smallest visible sunspots have an area of about 500 million square miles (1,300 million km^2), about fifty times the size of Africa. The largest sunspots have an area of about 7,000 million square miles (18,000 million km^2).

❏ The Sun gives off a stream of electrically-charged particles called the solar wind. Every second, the Sun pumps more than a million tons of material into the solar wind.

Darkness at noon – eclipses

On May 25, 585 B.C., in the Middle East, the forces of King Alyattes of the Lydians and King Cyaxares of the Medes were fighting an enormous battle. It was near sunset. Suddenly the sky darkened and, looking upward, the soldiers saw the Sun grow dim. It was an eclipse caused, we now know, by the Moon moving in front of the Sun. But to the frightened soldiers, it was a sign of the gods' displeasure. The two kings quickly made peace and hurried home. This eclipse is remembered for something more than stopping a battle; it was the first eclipse to be predicted beforehand, by the Greek philosopher Thales. Eclipses of the Sun – called solar eclipses – are caused by the Moon moving in front of the Sun. If the Moon is a little closer to the Earth in its orbit than usual, it can block out the Sun completely, causing a total eclipse. On other occasions, when the Moon is further away from the Earth, it does not completely block out the Sun. This results in a partial eclipse, or an annular eclipse, in which a ring of the Sun's outer edge is visible around the Moon. Eclipses of the Moon occur when the Moon moves into the shadow of the Earth. Since the positions of the Sun and Moon can be calculated, it is possible to predict when eclipses will occur. We know, for example, that there will be a total eclipse over central South America and part of the south Atlantic on November 3, 1994.

Artist's impression of Mayan people, who lived in the Yucatán Peninsula, Mexico, around A.D. 325-925, gathered for a religious ceremony during a total eclipse.

Artificially-colored photograph of a total eclipse of the Sun on February 26, 1979. The colors show the corona, the Sun's outer layer, which can only be seen during a total eclipse.

A total eclipse of the Sun (top) occurs when the Sun is completely obscured by the Moon. An annular eclipse (right) occurs when the Moon is slightly further from the Earth.

Total eclipse

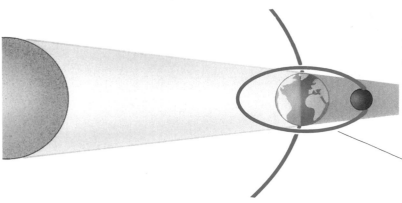

A lunar eclipse occurs when the Moon passes through the shadow of the Earth. This only happens at the time of a full Moon. During an eclipse, the Moon turns a dull copper color.

❏ The longest a total eclipse of the Sun can last is 7 minutes 31 seconds. An annular eclipse can last for 12 minutes 24 seconds. A lunar eclipse can last much longer: up to 104 minutes.

❏ The earliest recorded eclipse of the Sun was seen in China on October 22, 2136 B.C. The Chinese believed that eclipses were caused by a hungry dragon trying to eat the Sun. They also believed that the dragon could be scared away by making a terrible noise.

❏ The maximum number of eclipses that can occur in one year is seven. In 1935, for example, there were five solar eclipses and two lunar eclipses. In 1982 there were four solar eclipses and three lunar. The minimum number of eclipses that can occur in one year is two, both of which will be solar eclipses.

❏ In the near future total solar eclipses will occur on the following dates at the locations indicated.
November 3, 1994: Central S America, S Atlantic
October 24, 1995: S Asia, Central Pacific
March 9, 1997: Central Asia
February 26, 1998: Central Pacific, Northern S America
August 11, 1999: N Atlantic, Central Europe, S Asia

Annular
eclipse

The wonder of an eclipse is increased because the Moon cannot be seen approaching the Sun, and the eclipse happens without warning.

Exploring the planets

Unmanned spaceprobes have visited all the planets of the Solar System except Pluto, the smallest, most distant planet. Notable milestones have been the first craft to hit the Moon (Luna 2, 1959), the first soft landing on the Moon (Luna 9, 1966), the first flyby of another planet (Mariner 2 past Venus, 1962), the first craft to orbit another planet (Mariner 9 around Mars, 1971), the first photographs from the surface of Venus (Venera 9, 1975) and Mars (Viking 1, 1976), and the 'grand tour' by Voyager 2, which visited Jupiter, Saturn, Uranus, and Neptune. The Voyager 2 journey illustrates the extraordinary achievements needed to send probes to the distant planets. On August 25, 1989, Voyager 2 flew within 3,000 miles (4,800km) of Neptune, after a journey of 4,350 million miles (7,000 million km), at which time it was 2,750 million miles (4,400 million km) from Earth and traveling at 43,236mph (69,178km/h), 22 times faster than a bullet. This feat is like shooting a rifle bullet at a moving target, the size of a plum, a mile away and coming within a hair's breadth of hitting it. Its signal took 4 hours 6 minutes to reach Earth. The signal was transmitted at about the same power as a refrigerator light bulb. By the time the signal had reached the Earth, its strength was 20,000 million times weaker than the current from a tiny watch battery. Yet this minute signal was sufficient to carry to Earth breathtaking views of the distant planets.

Backdropped against the Earth and the blackness of space, the Galileo spacecraft is released from the Space Shuttle *Atlantis* on October 18, 1989. The craft is about to begin a six-year journey to Jupiter. On October 29, 1991 Galileo flew past the asteroid Gaspra at a distance of 10,000 miles (16,200km), the closest-ever approach to an asteroid.

The paths taken by Voyager 1 (orange track) and Voyager 2 (red track) on their exploratory trips to the outer planets.

The Pioneer Venus spacecraft are prepared for their flights to Venus. The orbiter and multiprobe craft arrived there in December 1978.

The Mariner 10 spacecraft undergoing tests prior to launch. The craft flew by Mercury in March 1974.

❏ By the time the Voyager 2 probe reached Uranus in 1986, its electronics and computers were completely out of date. They were designed in the early 1970s. By 1986 many people had more powerful microcomputers installed in their homes than were installed on Voyager.

❏ In January 1990, Pioneer 10, the first spacecraft to leave the Solar System, was 4,400 million miles (7,100 million km) from the Sun and was still returning data to Earth. It was traveling at 30,450mph (49,000km/h). In the year 34,593, Pioneer will fly by the star Ross 248 at a distance of 10 light-years.

❏ A rocket can reach the Moon in less time than it took to travel between cities by stage coach in the 19th century. On March 2, 1972, Pioneer 10 took off. It reached the Moon in half a day.

❏ The LAGEOS satellite – used to measure the Earth's shape – will stay in orbit for 8 million years. It carries engraved pictures to show future generations what life was like when it was launched.

❏ The first moon-shot, Luna 1, launched on January 2, 1959, missed its target by 3,700 miles (6,000km). Its speed was boosted by the pull of the Moon's gravity, and the probe ended up in orbit around the Sun. It will continue to circle the Sun for millions of years.

Mercury – planet of extremes

Mercury is a planet of extremes. It is the smallest of the planets, with the exception of Pluto. It mass is 20 times smaller than that of the Earth. Its diameter is a mere 3,032 miles (4,880km), a little over the distance from New York to San Francisco. Mercury is the planet closest to the Sun. On average Mercury is 36 million miles (58 million km) away from the Sun. This means that, viewed from the Earth, it is never far from the solar disk. It can be seen only near the horizon for a short time at dusk or dawn for a few weeks each year. Mercury is also the fastest-moving planet. It races around the Sun at an average speed of 107,030mph (172,248km/h), completing an orbit in 88 Earth days. This means that a year on Mercury only lasts 88 Earth days. As it moves around the Sun, Mercury is slowly spinning. It spins more slowly than any planet other than Venus. This means that its days and nights are very long. A day or night on Mercury lasts 59 times longer than a day or night on Earth. This means that the planet experiences extremes of temperature; during the day, temperatures can reach 662°F (350°C), over seven times hotter than the hottest desert on Earth. At night, the temperature can drop to −274°F (−170°C), about eight times colder than the temperature inside a home freezer.

A temperature map of Mercury made from radio observations undertaken by the Very Large Array radio telescope, Socorro, New Mexico. The colors show the temperature just below the planet's surface, red indicating the highest temperature of 260°F (127°C).

A mosaic of Mariner 10 photographs of Mercury, showing its heavily cratered surface. The planet is named after the Roman deity who was the messenger of the gods.

An artist's impression of sunrise on Mercury. The surface is a copper-colored version of our own Moon.

❏ Mercury has a core of iron about the size of the Moon. If this could be mined, it would supply enough iron to meet our needs on Earth for thousands of millions of years.

❏ The atmosphere of Mercury is almost non-existent. To fill a child's party balloon would take all the gas from a volume of the atmosphere measuring 2 miles (3.2km) by 2 miles by 2 miles.

❏ Mercury can be seen in the eastern sky close to the horizon just before sunrise (as above) on the following dates.
1993: April 5, August 4, November 22
1994: March 19, July 17, November 6
1995: March 1, June 29, October 20
1996: February 11, June 10, October 3

❏ Mercury can be seen in the western sky just after sunset on the following dates:
1993: February 21, June 17, October 14
1994: February 4, May 30, September 26
1995: January 19, May 12, September 9
1996: January 2, April 23, August 21, December 15

Venus – the cloudy planet

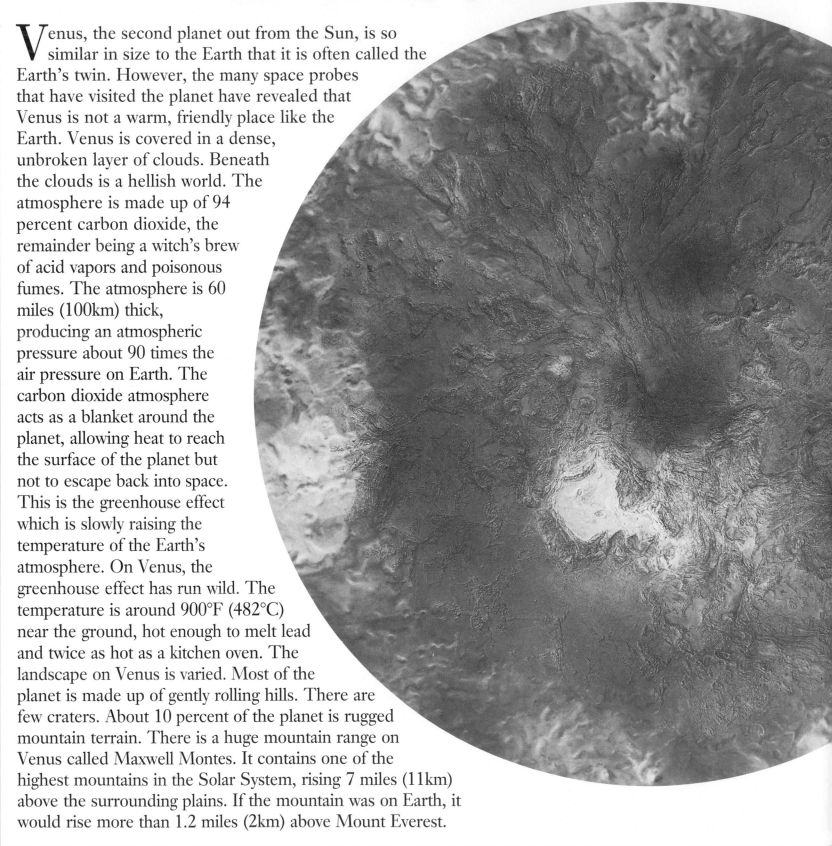

Venus, the second planet out from the Sun, is so similar in size to the Earth that it is often called the Earth's twin. However, the many space probes that have visited the planet have revealed that Venus is not a warm, friendly place like the Earth. Venus is covered in a dense, unbroken layer of clouds. Beneath the clouds is a hellish world. The atmosphere is made up of 94 percent carbon dioxide, the remainder being a witch's brew of acid vapors and poisonous fumes. The atmosphere is 60 miles (100km) thick, producing an atmospheric pressure about 90 times the air pressure on Earth. The carbon dioxide atmosphere acts as a blanket around the planet, allowing heat to reach the surface of the planet but not to escape back into space. This is the greenhouse effect which is slowly raising the temperature of the Earth's atmosphere. On Venus, the greenhouse effect has run wild. The temperature is around 900°F (482°C) near the ground, hot enough to melt lead and twice as hot as a kitchen oven. The landscape on Venus is varied. Most of the planet is made up of gently rolling hills. There are few craters. About 10 percent of the planet is rugged mountain terrain. There is a huge mountain range on Venus called Maxwell Montes. It contains one of the highest mountains in the Solar System, rising 7 miles (11km) above the surrounding plains. If the mountain was on Earth, it would rise more than 1.2 miles (2km) above Mount Everest.

Magellan arrived at Venus on August 10, 1990, and transmitted its first pictures on August 16, 1990. Magellan orbited Venus about once every three hours, mapping the surface by radar.

Color-coded map of Venus' north pole. Yellow areas represent high ground and orange areas low ground. The yellow area just below center contains the Maxwell Montes, the highest mountains on Venus.

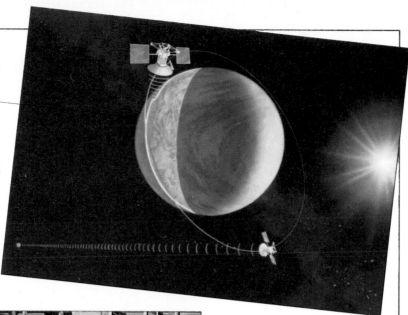

❏ The planet Venus is named after the Roman goddess of love.

❏ Napoleon Bonaparte, the French Emperor between 1804 and 1815, was once upstaged by the planet Venus. During a visit to Luxemburg, the crowd at a rally was more interested in watching the planet which was visible in the noontime sky than in listening to Napoleon.

❏ Venus is much brighter than any other planet or star. At its brightest it can cast shadows, and even be seen during the day time.

Engineers prepare the Magellan spacecraft for its journey to Venus. Magellan was released from the Space Shuttle *Atlantis* on May 4, 1989. During its 15-month cruise, the craft traveled 93 million miles (150 million km).

❏ To see Venus, try looking in the western sky just after sunset during the first half of the year; during the second half of the year, Venus can be seen in the eastern sky before dawn. Good dates to watch out are:
1993: January 19, June 10
1994: August 25
1995: January 13
1996: April 1, August 19

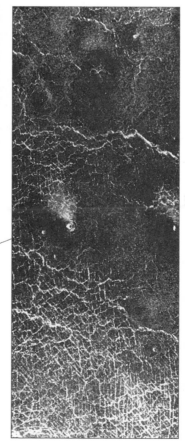

❏ On Venus, the Sun rises in the west and sets in the east, the opposite of Earth. This is because Venus rotates from east to west, not from west to east as the Earth and the other planets do.

Magellan radar image of the surface of Venus showing signs of active volcanoes. The crater in the center of the image has a fan of material stretching upward about 6 miles (10km). It is probably a surface deposit.

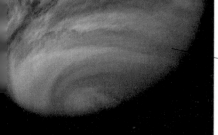

Ultraviolet view of Venus' clouds taken by the Pioneer Venus probe. The planet's clouds circle Venus once every four hours. The cloud cover shows circular patterns similar to cloud patterns seen on Earth.

❏ Venus is the planet that turns most slowly on its axis. It spins once every 243 Earth days. Since Venus takes 224 Earth days to complete one orbit of the Sun, its days are longer than its years.

Mars – the red planet

Ever since the late 1800s, some astronomers have believed that life might be found on Mars. Italian astronomer Giovanni Schiaparelli in 1877 drew a map of the planet based on telescopic observations showing long, straight channels or canals apparently built by intelligent beings. In 1894, Percival Lowell founded an observatory at Flagstaff, Arizona, to study the canals. He believed they might be the work of living creatures struggling to survive in an inhospitable environment. However, belief in the canals was finally overturned in 1965 when Mars was visited by the Mariner 4 space probe. This craft flew by the planet, transmitting 22 pictures back to Earth. The pictures showed a lifeless world. True, the planet had channels but they seemed to be dry stream beds rather than constructed canals. In July 1976, two U.S. space probes – Viking 1 and 2 – soft landed on the Martian surface. Color television pictures transmitted to Earth revealed why the planet can be called the 'red planet:' the Martian sky is pink, colored by iron oxide dust blown in the atmosphere. Other experiments on the Viking craft showed that the atmosphere was thin, only one-hundredth that of Earth. It is mainly carbon dioxide but because the atmosphere is so thin, there is no greenhouse effect on Mars. The temperature on the equator of Mars can rise as high as 80°F (27°C) during the day, and drop as low as −167°F (−111°C) at night.

A mosaic of photographs taken by the Viking spacecraft orbiting above Mars. The image shows the Candor Chasm, part of Mars' giant Valles Marineris canyon system. In this region, the canyon is about 62 miles (100km) wide and up to 5 miles (8km) deep.

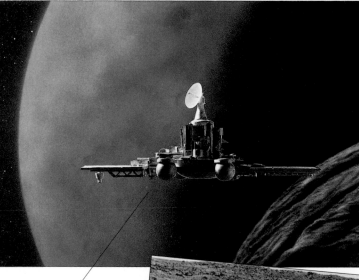

Artist's impression of the Phobos spaceprobe making its final approach to Phobos, the larger of the two small Martian moons. The dark spot at top center is one of Mars' large, extinct volcanoes.

The Martian landscape, as seen from the Viking 1 lander. The robot arm, which scooped up soil for analysis by equipment installed on the probe, can be seen. Disappointingly, the samples revealed no signs of life.

Viking orbiter photograph showing white water mist within the Valles Marineris' canyons. Most of the water in Mars' atmosphere comes from the north polar cap.

Sunset over Mars, photographed by Viking 1. The sky is tinted by dust in the atmosphere.

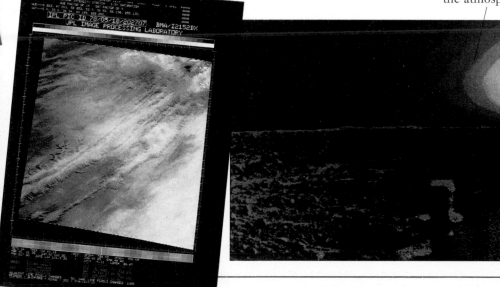

❑ The atmosphere of Mars is relatively moist. However, because the atmosphere is thin, the total amount of water in the atmosphere is small. If all the water in the atmosphere of Mars was collected, it would only fill a small pond.

❑ The moons of Mars are called Phobos (Greek for fear) and Deimos (Greek for panic) after two mythical horses that drew the chariot of Mars, the god of war.

❑ The largest crater on Mars' moon Phobos is named Stickney after the wife of the discoverer of the two Martian moons, American astronomer Asaph Hall. In 1877 she persuaded her discouraged husband to continue his search for the moons for just one more night. The very next night, the moons were found.

❑ Deimos, a tiny moon circling Mars, has very weak gravity. Fast runners could launch themselves into space simply by reaching a speed of 22mph (36km/h) – the fastest humans can reach around 27 mph (43 km/h), and so would have no trouble getting spaceborne.

❑ A giant canyon called Valles Marineris (Mariner Valley) stretches across Mars. It is 2,500 miles (4,000km) long – 13 times longer than the Grand Canyon – and would stretch from San Francisco to New York. In places the valley is 124 miles (200km) wide and 4 miles (7km) deep.

Jupiter – the giant planet

The outer planets, Jupiter, Saturn, Uranus, and Neptune, are giant balls of gas. They differ from the inner planets which are smaller rocky bodies. Jupiter is by far the largest of the planets. It is more than 11 times larger in diameter than the Earth; it could contain 1,323 Earths inside its volume. All the planets of the Solar System would fit inside a hollow Jupiter. Jupiter is so big that a motorist driving at a constant 60mph (100km/h) would take 187 days to travel around the planet. Deep within Jupiter, there is probably a solid core, about 15 times more massive than the Earth. This core is surrounded by solid hydrogen, compressed by the immense pressure of the atmosphere. The pressure at Jupiter's center is 100 million times higher than the Earth's air pressure. Anyone trying to land on Jupiter would be crushed long before they reached the solid core of the planet. Above the core, there is a layer of liquid hydrogen covered by a gaseous atmosphere, 620 miles (1,000km) thick, consisting mainly of hydrogen and helium, with traces of hydrogen compounds such as ammonia and methane. The outer layer of the atmosphere is very cold, about −400°F (−240°C), while lower layers can be as hot as 80°F (27°C). At the center of Jupiter, the temperature is about 54,000°F (30,000°C).

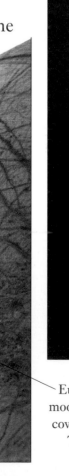

Jupiter and two of its 16 moons, photographed from a distance of 17 million miles (28 million km) by Voyager 1 on February 5, 1979. Jupiter's innermost moon, Io, can be seen against the planet's disk. At the far right is Europa. The planet's atmosphere consists of colorful, swirling bands of cloud.

The moon, Io, has many active volcanoes showing here as dark spots. The whitish areas are solid sulfur dioxide, produced by the volcanoes.

The long, curved marks on the surface of Europa stretch for thousands of miles across its surface. They seem to be fractures in its crust.

Europa, one of Jupiter's large moons. The surface of Europa is covered by long, dark markings. They may be cracks in the surface, filled with ice.

Jupiter's Great Red Spot, a massive storm in the thick atmosphere, shown to scale with the Earth.

A Voyager 2 picture of Ganymede, Jupiter's largest moon. The bright spots on the surface are impact craters. The dark area is called Galileo Regio.

❏ The planet Jupiter is named after the supreme god of the Romans. He was the god of the sky, the bringer of light, hurling lightning bolts down on the world when displeased.

❏ Jupiter spins faster than any other planet. A point on the equator of Jupiter spins around the center of the planet at a speed of 28,273mph (45,500km/h). The speed of the spin makes the planet bulge slightly at its equator.

❏ On Jupiter, your weight would be nearly three times greater than it is on Earth.

❏ Jupiter is the planet with the shortest day: slightly under 10 hours. However, its year is 12 times as long as one of ours.

❏ Ganymede, Jupiter's largest satellite, is actually larger than the planet Mercury. It is 3,275 miles (5,270km) in diameter.

❏ Jupiter is much smaller than the Sun. If the Sun was the size of a basket ball, 1ft (30cm) across, Jupiter would be the size of a table tennis ball, 1in (4cm) across. On this scale, the Earth would be less than 0.1in (2.5mm) across.

❏ One of Jupiter's moons, called J3, is the fastest moving moon in the Solar System. It is only 25 miles (40km) across, and moves at a speed of 70,400mph (113,300km/h), fast enough to take it from San Francisco to New York in 2 minutes 15 seconds.

Saturn – the ringed planet

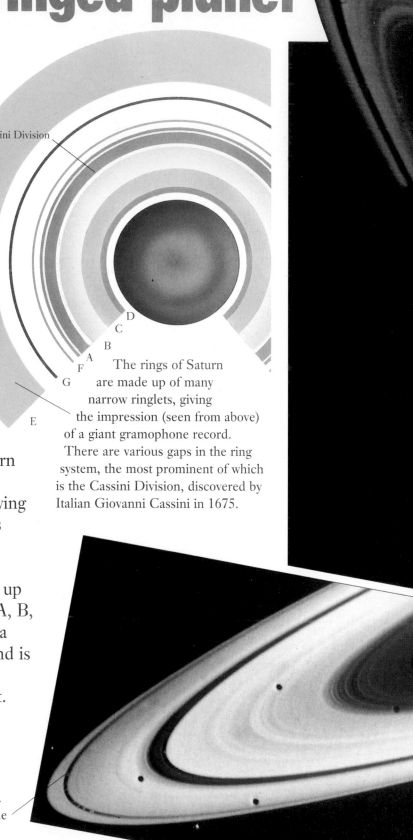

Saturn is the sixth planet out from the Sun, orbiting at an average distance of 886 million miles (1,427 million km). It is the second largest planet with an equatorial diameter of 74,500 miles (120,000km). The volume of Saturn is 815 times that of the Earth. In some ways, Saturn is like a smaller version of Jupiter. It has a small solid core, surrounded by a layer of liquid hydrogen and a hydrogen-rich atmosphere. It has a turbulent upper atmosphere, and cloud movements are more violent than on Jupiter. However, Saturn has two claims to uniqueness: it is the planet with most satellites or moons, and it has the most spectacular system of rings. Saturn has 21-23 moons; the exact number is uncertain because of difficulties in identifying the individual moons. The largest moon is Titan, with a diameter of 3,200 miles (5,150km), about half the diameter of the Earth. The rings around Saturn are made up of three main bright regions, called rings A, B, and C. The outermost bright ring, A, has a diameter of 170,000 miles (272,000km) and is separated from ring B by a gap called the Cassini Division. The inner ring C is faint. Within the rings, there are many smaller gaps and other features like spokes or twisted strands.

Cassini Division

The rings of Saturn are made up of many narrow ringlets, giving the impression (seen from above) of a giant gramophone record. There are various gaps in the ring system, the most prominent of which is the Cassini Division, discovered by Italian Giovanni Cassini in 1675.

Newly discovered small moons near the rings of Saturn. It is thought that these moons play a part in stabilizing the rings. They act as 'shepherds,' keeping the rings from breaking up.

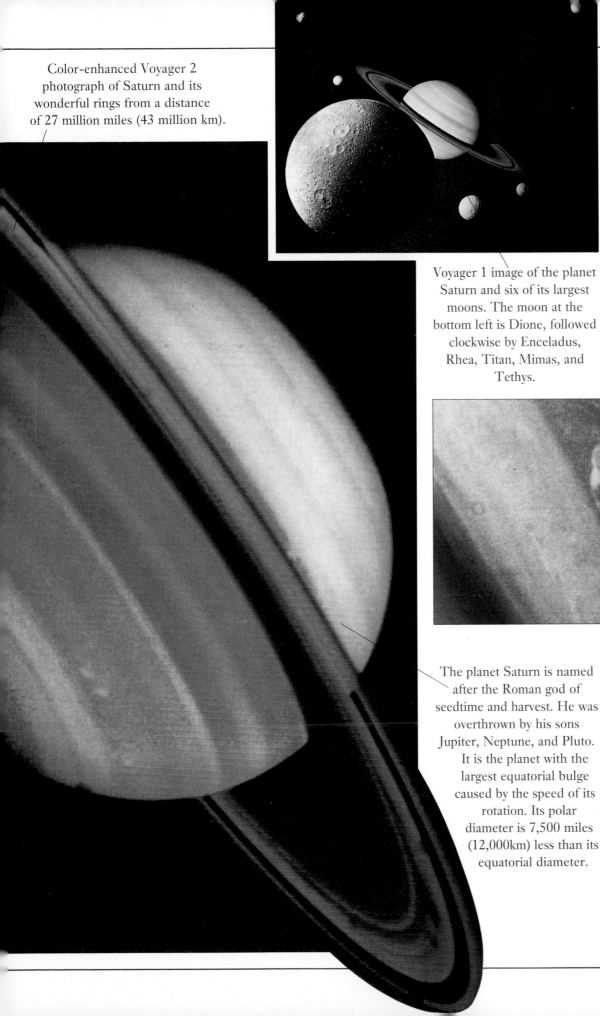

Color-enhanced Voyager 2 photograph of Saturn and its wonderful rings from a distance of 27 million miles (43 million km).

Voyager 1 image of the planet Saturn and six of its largest moons. The moon at the bottom left is Dione, followed clockwise by Enceladus, Rhea, Titan, Mimas, and Tethys.

The planet Saturn is named after the Roman god of seedtime and harvest. He was overthrown by his sons Jupiter, Neptune, and Pluto. It is the planet with the largest equatorial bulge caused by the speed of its rotation. Its polar diameter is 7,500 miles (12,000km) less than its equatorial diameter.

FACT FILE

❏ The year on Saturn is 29½ times longer than ours, but its day is shorter than ours, 11½ hours.

❏ The Earth is the most dense planet – five times denser than water, while Saturn is the least dense. It has a density of only 0.7 times that of water. Saturn would float in water if there was an ocean large enough to accommodate it. However, Saturn is 95 times heavier than the Earth.

❏ Winds ten times stronger than a hurricane on Earth blow around Saturn's equator. Wind speeds can reach 1,100mph (1,770km/h).

❏ The rings of Saturn are very thin compared to their width. They are only 300ft (100m) thick but 171,000 miles (275,000km) in diameter. If a scale model was made of the planet and its rings, and was constructed of thin cardboard, the rings would measure 4 miles (6.5km) from their inner edge to the outer edge.

The outer planets – Uranus, Neptune, Pluto

The planets Uranus, Neptune, and Pluto lie on the outer edge of the Solar System. Uranus lies at an average distance of 1,780 million miles (2,865 million km) from the Sun, about 19 times farther from the Sun than the Earth. If the Concorde supersonic aircraft flew to Uranus at its usual cruising speed of 1,350mph (2,170km/h), the journey from Earth to Uranus would last 150 years. Neptune lies at an average distance of 2,800 million miles (4,500 million km) from the Sun, about 30 times farther from the Sun than the Earth. Pluto lies at an average distance of 3,670 million miles (5,900 million km), about 39 times farther from the Sun than the Earth. Uranus and Neptune are gas giants like Saturn and Neptune. They are the third and fourth largest planets; even so, their masses are only about one-twentieth of that of Jupiter. The oddest feature of Uranus is that it is tipped on its side so that each pole is sometimes pointed at the Sun. The polar regions are warmer than the equator. At the poles, a day lasts for 42 Earth years, followed by an equally long night. Neptune is very similar to Uranus; the two planets are roughly the same size and mass. Both have faint ring systems. Pluto barely qualifies as a planet. It is smaller than our Moon, only 1,500 miles (2,400km) across and only 0.002 times as heavy as the Earth. Perhaps it was once a moon of Neptune. It has one claim to fame, however. Pluto has the most elongated orbit of all the planets. Because of this, during the period 1979 to 1999, Pluto actually passes inside the orbit of Neptune and is closer to the Sun than Neptune for that time.

Pluto and its moon, Charon. Pluto was discovered in 1930 by Clyde Tombaugh at the Lowell Observatory, Flagstaff, Arizona. Charon was discovered in 1978 by James Christy at the Naval Observatory, Flagstaff.

Two Voyager 2 images of Uranus taken in January 1986. The images are colored to bring out details in the polar region (marked by a circle on the right-hand image).

Artist's impression of the planet Neptune seen from its large moon, Triton. A geyser of liquid methane is erupting from Triton's surface, which consists of a layer of frozen methane and nitrogen.

Voyager 2 view of Neptune. Objects that are deep in the atmosphere are colored blue, while those at higher altitudes are white. The bright, white feature is a high-altitude cloud. A long narrow band of cloud runs across the northern region.

❑ Urbain Le Verrier, the French astronomer who predicted the existence of Neptune, was sacked from his position of director of the Paris Observatory in 1870 because of his rudeness. It was said of him that he may not have been the most detestable man in France, but he was the most detested! He got his post back when his successor was drowned in a boating accident.

❑ The planet Uranus was discovered on March 13, 1781 by William Herschel with a telescope situated in his garden in the city of Bath, England. At this time Herschel was an amateur astronomer, his chosen profession being music-making.

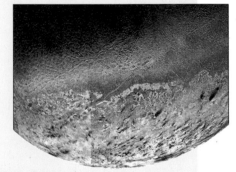

❑ The coldest place in the Solar System is the surface of Neptune's largest moon Triton (seen above), which has temperature of −391°F (−235°C), only 69°F (38°C) above absolute zero.

❑ The average surface temperature of the outer planets – Uranus, Neptune, Pluto – is about −364°F (−220°C), 11 times colder than inside a home freezer.

Asteroids – space debris

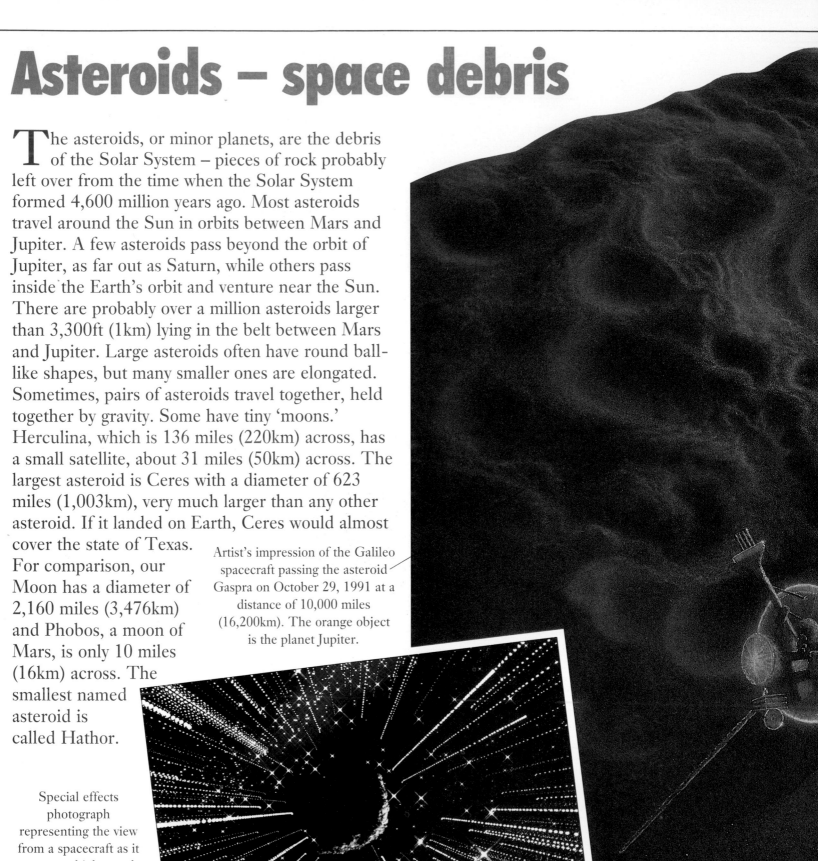

The asteroids, or minor planets, are the debris of the Solar System – pieces of rock probably left over from the time when the Solar System formed 4,600 million years ago. Most asteroids travel around the Sun in orbits between Mars and Jupiter. A few asteroids pass beyond the orbit of Jupiter, as far out as Saturn, while others pass inside the Earth's orbit and venture near the Sun. There are probably over a million asteroids larger than 3,300ft (1km) lying in the belt between Mars and Jupiter. Large asteroids often have round ball-like shapes, but many smaller ones are elongated. Sometimes, pairs of asteroids travel together, held together by gravity. Some have tiny 'moons.' Herculina, which is 136 miles (220km) across, has a small satellite, about 31 miles (50km) across. The largest asteroid is Ceres with a diameter of 623 miles (1,003km), very much larger than any other asteroid. If it landed on Earth, Ceres would almost cover the state of Texas. For comparison, our Moon has a diameter of 2,160 miles (3,476km) and Phobos, a moon of Mars, is only 10 miles (16km) across. The smallest named asteroid is called Hathor.

Artist's impression of the Galileo spacecraft passing the asteroid Gaspra on October 29, 1991 at a distance of 10,000 miles (16,200km). The orange object is the planet Jupiter.

Special effects photograph representing the view from a spacecraft as it passes at high speed through the asteroid belt. The blue band at the upper left is the Milky Way.

Artist's impression of the asteroid Hidalgo (top) during a close approach to Jupiter and its moons. Hidalgo has an unusual orbit, traveling out past Jupiter almost as far as Saturn.

Most asteroids orbit between Mars and Jupiter, held in position by Jupiter's gravity. There is at least one gap in the asteroid belt, known as the Kirkwood gap. Two groups of asteroids, called the Trojans, precede and follow Jupiter around in its orbit.

❏ In 1800 a group of astronomers in Germany formed a society to hunt for an undiscovered planet thought to be situated between the orbits of Mars and Jupiter. They called themselves the Celestial Police. The Police did not make the first 'arrest' – the first asteroid, Ceres, was discovered by Italian Giuseppe Piazzi in 1801. The Police discovered three asteroids (Pallas, Juno, and Vesta) between 1802 and 1807, and finally disbanded in 1815. The next asteroid was not found until 1845.

❏ The brightest asteroid is called Vesta. It has a diameter of 335 miles (540km) and is the only asteroid visible to the unaided eye.

❏ When an asteroid is discovered, it is given an identification number. Then the discoverer of the asteroid is allowed the honor of naming it. Over the years, asteroids have been named after a calculator (asteroid 1625, the NORC, or Naval Ordnance Research Calculator at Dahlgren, Virginia), musical plays (1047 the Geisha), shipping lines (724 Hapag, or Hamburg Amerika Line), flowers (978 Petunia), and a sweet that the discoverer was fond of (518 Halawa, an Arabian sweet).

❏ In 1937 the tiny asteroid Hermes passed uncomfortably close to the Earth, at a distance of less than twice that of the Moon.

Long-haired stars – comets

Artificially-colored image of Comet West, taken on March 8, 1976, showing the comet's twin tails. As Comet West receded from the Earth, it broke into four pieces. It is expected to return to Earth in 300,000 years' time – if it has not disintegrated completely in the meantime.

Artificially-colored image of Comet Bradfield as seen by the International Ultraviolet Explorer satellite in 1980. The comet was visible, at its brightest, with the unaided eye and sported a long tail. It was named after its discoverer, Australian Bill Bradfield.

Comets have long been popularly known as 'long-haired stars.' The Greek word 'kometes' in fact means long-haired. In A.D. 79, the Roman emperor Vespasian, observing a comet in the sky, remarked that it was a bad sign for his enemy, the King of the Parthians, 'for he is hairy, while I am bald.' In fact, comets are not stars, and they are not hairy! Comets appear as fuzzy patches of light, sometimes with long tails, which are seen in the night sky from time to time. Some comets, called periodics, appear at regular intervals. Halley's comet, for example, appears every 76 years. Most comets, however, appear only once. If they ever return to Earth, it will be in thousands of millions of years. More than 700 comets have been observed. About six new ones are discovered each year. It has been estimated that around 100,000 million comets may circle around the Sun. Comets are members of the Solar System. They orbit around the Sun. However, their orbits are very elongated, not nearly circular like the orbits of the planets. Comets are probably balls of icy material; they have been called 'dirty snowballs.' When comets come close to the Sun, some of the ice is vaporized to form a long stream or tail.

Artist's impression of a cometary nucleus approaching the Sun. Each time a comet approaches the Sun, ices and frozen gases on its surface begin to evaporate and form a long tail.

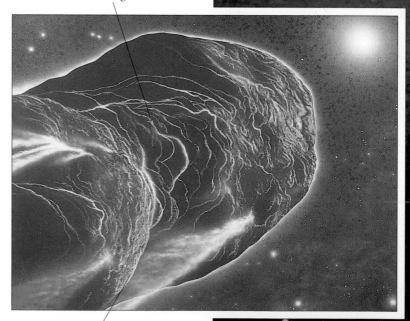

On each journey around the Sun, a comet loses some of its mass. Eventually, only the dark, rocky nucleus remains. The comet will be unseen when it next passes the Earth.

A comet's tail always points away from the Sun, blown by the solar wind, a stream of energetic particles flowing outward from the Sun. A comet's tail is easily blown about as it contains very little solid matter. It may stretch for millions of miles through space.

FACT FILE

❏ French astronomer Charles Messier spent a lifetime hunting for comets. He claimed to have discovered 21 of them. King Louis XV of France called him the 'comet ferret.' Messier is best known today for a catalog published in 1781 listing over 100 dim, hazy nebulae – objects to avoid when comet hunting.

❏ Portuguese wine bottled in 1811 is called 'comet wine.' Its excellent quality is believed to be due to the Great Comet of that year. The term 'comet wine' is often used for any wine made in the year of an important comet.

❏ Comets speed up as they approach the Sun – sometimes reaching speeds of over a million mph (1.6 million km/h). Far away from the Sun, speeds drop, perhaps down to as little as 700mph (1,125km/h).

❏ The Earth's most frequent visitor is Encke's comet which returns to our planet each 1,206 days. It has been seen 54 times, but is growing increasingly faint. It is expected to have completely faded by February 1994, its next scheduled return.

Giotto – mission to Halley's comet

Edmond Halley (1656-1742), an English astronomer who showed that comets move around the Sun in elliptical orbits.

Halley's comet, photographed on May 25, 1910, from Helwan, Egypt. It returns to Earth every 76 years and has been observed and recorded for more than 3,000 years.

In March 1986, Halley's comet was visited by six spacecraft from Earth. Two Japanese craft – Sakigake and Suisei – and the U.S. ICE craft flew ahead of the comet, gathering data about conditions upstream of the comet. Two Soviet craft – Vega 1 and Vega 2 – flew to within 5,600 miles (9,000km) of the comet. The European Space Agency's probe called Giotto made the closest approach, flying to within 335 miles (540km) of the comet's core on March 13, 1986. The nucleus of Halley's comet was revealed to be a peanut-shaped object, weighing about 100,000 million tons (91,000 million tonnes) and measuring about 9 miles by 5 miles (15km by 8km). It was made up of dirty ice. As the craft flew by the comet, dust and particles in the cometary tail smashed into the craft at speeds up to 150,000mph (240,000km/h). Despite the craft's dust shields, the collisions damaged the camera, battery, and other key parts, and Giotto fell silent. Twenty-one seconds later miraculously it came back to life. It had lost some of its equipment, and only half its instruments were working. Nevertheless, Giotto limped on through space. It had not been destroyed by the encounter as scientists had feared. Taking advantage of the good luck, ground control on Earth transmitted new instructions, and Giotto set out on a second mission: to visit a comet called Grigg-Skjellerup that orbits the Sun every five years. When Giotto reaches its new target, it will no doubt be damaged further. Its useful life will then surely be over.

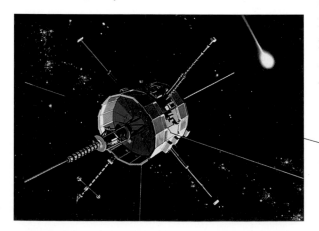

NASA's ICE (International Cometary Explorer) spacecraft was launched in 1978. On September 11, 1985, it flew through the tail of Comet Giacobini-Zinner.

Giotto's payload included a camera, three instruments for analyzing the chemical composition of the comet, and dust impact detectors. The information gathered was transmitted back to Earth at the rate of 40,000 pieces of data per second.

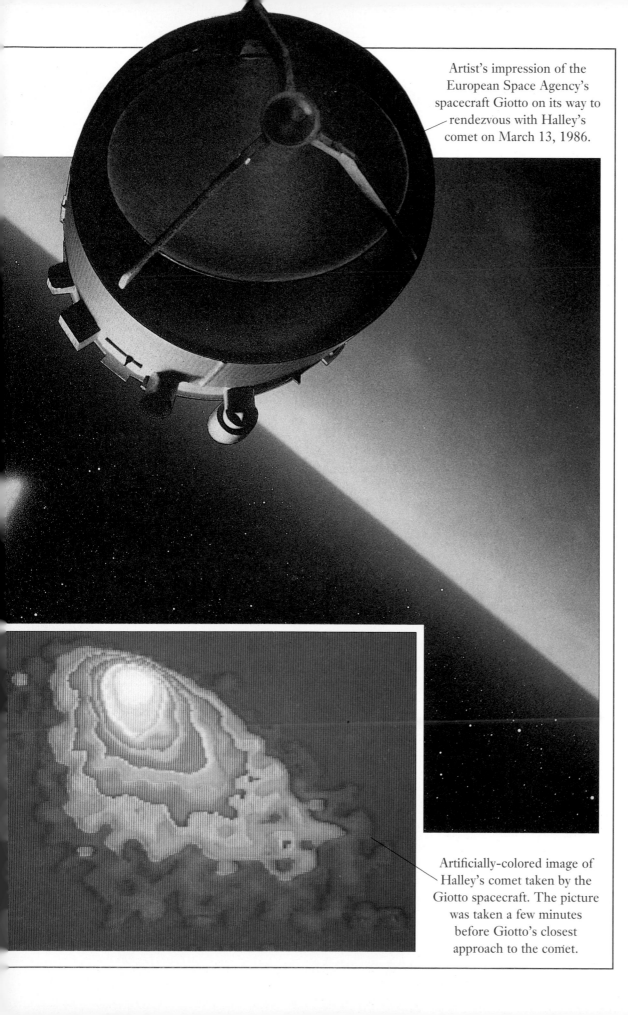

Artist's impression of the European Space Agency's spacecraft Giotto on its way to rendezvous with Halley's comet on March 13, 1986.

Artificially-colored image of Halley's comet taken by the Giotto spacecraft. The picture was taken a few minutes before Giotto's closest approach to the comet.

❏ In 1066 Halley's comet appeared shortly before William the Conqueror invaded England. The Norman king took it as a good omen; his battle cry became 'A new star, a new king.'

❏ The *Anglo-Saxon Chronicle* records the 1066 visit of Halley's comet: 'Then there was seen all over England a sign such as no one had ever seen. Some said that the star was a comet, as some called the long-haired star. It had a tail streaming like smoke up to nearly half the sky.'

❏ In 1456, Halley's comet appeared while Christians and Turks were at war. Pope Callistus III officially cursed the comet, declaring it the work of the devil. The Pope may have been a little too hasty. During the battle of Belgrade, later in the same year, the comet's long tail, looking like a drawn sword, was seen to be pointing toward the Turks. This so heartened the Christians that they launched an attack that won the battle.

❏ In 1910, when Halley's comet could again be seen, a businessman in America made a fortune by selling 'anti-comet' pills.

❏ The Giotto spacecraft was named after the Italian painter Giotto di Bondone who in 1304 painted Halley's comet as the 'Star of Bethlehem' as part of a fresco painting in a chapel at Padua, Italy.

Missiles from space

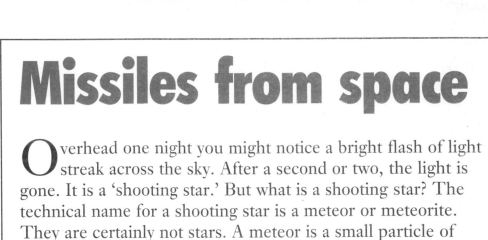

Overhead one night you might notice a bright flash of light streak across the sky. After a second or two, the light is gone. It is a 'shooting star.' But what is a shooting star? The technical name for a shooting star is a meteor or meteorite. They are certainly not stars. A meteor is a small particle of dust that falls from space and burns up in the upper atmosphere. The average meteor is no larger than a grain of sand. It has been estimated that 75 million meteors enter the atmosphere each day. Under ideal conditions, it should be possible to see about 10 meteors per hour with the unaided eye. A meteorite is a larger piece of space debris that survives its journey through Earth's atmosphere and actually hits the ground. A meteorite is larger than a meteor so it does not completely burn up as it falls to the ground. The largest known meteorite was found near Hoba West, near Grootfontein in Namibia in 1920. It was 9ft (2.75m) long and weighed 130,000lb (59 tonnes), as much as 15 elephants. It is estimated that more than 19,000 meteorites heavier than 3½oz (100g) land each year. Most of these fall in the oceans. About 150 meteorites fall each year on to the land surface of the Earth. Fewer than 10 are found and studied by scientists.

Old print of the Great Meteor Shower of November 12-13, 1833, as seen at Niagara Falls. The print shows that the meteor showers radiate out from a single point, called the radiant. Many meteors arrive in showers like this.

Aerial view of Barringer Crater, near Winslow, Arizona. The crater, caused by a meteorite impact about 50,000 years ago, is about 575ft (175m) deep and 3,940ft (1,200m) across.

Artist's impression of an incoming meteor. Meteors arrive at high speeds and burn up in the upper atmosphere, 60 miles (80km) high.

Meteorite recovered from the Elephant Moraine region of Antarctica by U.S. scientists in 1979. This 15-pound (6.8kg) rock is about 1,300 million years old. It is mainly composed of basalt, and originated as debris from another meteor impact on Mars.

Microscope photograph of a meteorite. Meteorites are made of fragments formed by collisions between asteroids orbiting the Sun in a belt between Mars and Jupiter. The fragments resulting from the collisions are deflected into orbits that cross the path of the Earth.

Journey to the stars

Is travel to the stars an impossible dream? Certainly, the distances between the stars and galaxies are vast. Even traveling at the speed of light – 186,281 miles per second (299,782km/sec) – we would take over 4 years to reach the star nearest to Earth. At the speed of light, it would take over 2 million years to reach the Andromeda galaxy, the closest large galaxy to ours. Could we travel faster than light? Alas, this is not possible. The great German scientist Albert Einstein discovered in 1905 that the speed of light is the ultimate speed limit. Nothing can travel faster than light. In fact, no material body can even reach the speed of light. The reason, according to Einstein's theory of relativity, is that the mass of an object increases as its speed increases. This make it harder and harder for the object to accelerate as its speed gets greater. Albert Einstein made another remarkable discovery: time slows down when a spaceship moves at speeds close to the speed of light. Imagine that an astronaut has left Earth traveling at 90 percent of the speed of light. The astronaut would not notice anything strange but to us, left on Earth, the effects of the high speed would be very noticeable. The mass of the spacecraft would double, and a clock on board would take an hour to record 26 minutes because time would have slowed. The astronaut would age at half the rate of a twin left behind on Earth. This is a sort of time travel. The astronaut, arriving back on Earth, would think that he had traveled into the future! Unfortunately, such calculations are all theoretical, and travel to the stars will probably remain a dream.

A particle accelerator at DESY, the German particle physics laboratory in Hamburg. Within particle accelerators, sub-atomic particles travel at near light-speed, but no object can ever reach light-speed. It is Nature's ultimate speed limit.

The design of a plate attached to the Pioneer 10 spacecraft, indicating its origin in case the craft should one day be found by another intelligent species. In 1983, Pioneer 10 became the first spacecraft to leave the Solar System. It is heading deeper into space.

Artist's impression of a space station that could house 10,000 people. It would rotate slowly to provide artificial gravity. The circular shield protects against dangerous radiation.

Astronauts in a space station are weightless. They sleep in bags secured to their bedroom walls, and move around inside the station by gripping on to hand-holds attached to the station's walls.

Artist's impression of a spaceship arriving at the moon of giant planet orbiting another star. Generations of crew members would live and die on the ship during the journey to the stars.

FACT FILE

❑ If our Sun was only 1in (2.5cm) across, the star nearest to Earth would be 445 miles (716km) away. On this scale, the most distant star in our Galaxy would be over 8 million miles (13 million km) away. The nearest large neighboring galaxy, the Andromeda galaxy, would be 227 million miles (360 million km) away.

❑ Life might exist on other planets in space. Traces of amino acids, which are the chemical building blocks of life, have been found in some meteorites.

❑ The Voyager 2 spacecraft carried a 12in (31cm) gold-plated record, a greeting to the Universe called 'The Sounds of Earth,' together with a record player and instructions on how to play the record – just in case the craft was picked up by an alien race in the depths of space.

❑ Light takes . . . 4.3 years to travel from the nearest star, Proxima Centauri to Earth . . . 75,000 years to travel from the most distant stars in our Galaxy . . . 160,000 years to travel from the nearest small galaxy, the Larger Magellanic Cloud . . . 2,200,000 years to travel from the nearest large galaxy, the Andromeda galaxy . . . more than 13,000,000,000 years to travel from the most distant objects in the Universe, quasars.

The nearest stars

The Sun is the nearest star to Earth. To us this now seems obvious, but the realization that the Sun is an ordinary star was one of the great insights of astronomy. To ancient Greek, Babylonian, or Egyptian astronomers, the Sun seemed very different from the faint points of light seen in the night sky. Apart from the Sun, the nearest bright star to us is called Alpha Centauri. This star lies in the southern skies, close to the constellation of Crux, or the Southern Cross. Alpha Centauri is 4.3 light-years, or 25 million million miles (40 million million km) away. Light takes 4.3 years to reach us from Alpha Centauri. Alpha Centauri differs from the Sun in one major respect. It is not a single star – it consists of three stars orbiting around each other. The two brightest stars, called A and B, circle around each other every 80 years. The third star is called Proxima Centauri since it is the closest to Earth of the three (after the Latin word *proximus* meaning near). It is a small star, about one-tenth the mass of the Sun, and orbits around A and B every million years. The next nearest star is called Barnard's star, in honor of Edward Barnard, the American astronomer who discovered it. Barnard's star lies at a distance of 5.9 light-years from Earth. It has a unique distinction: it changes its position in the sky – relative to other stars – more rapidly than any other star.

The nearest stars. Alpha Centauri (center left) is a triple star system. The two brightest components, A and B, circle around each other. The third component, Proxima Centauri, is the closest known star. Beta Centauri (center) is a more remote blue-white giant star.

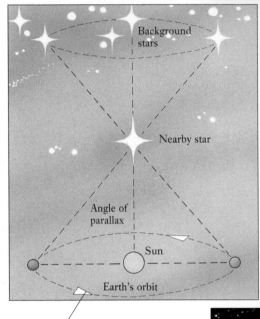

The distance to a nearby star can be found by observing its apparent movement against background stars as the Earth orbits the Sun. The closer a star is, the more it appears to move.

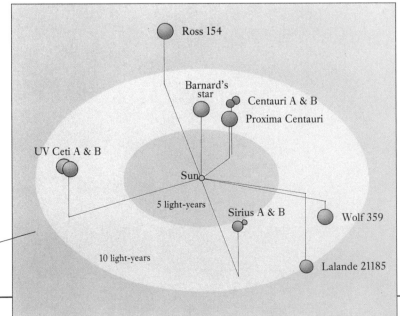

The stars within 10 light-years of the Sun. Of these stars, only two, Sirius and Alpha Centauri, are visible to the naked eye. Sirius is the brightest star in the sky.

Surveyors find the distance to a far-away hill by measuring the direction to the hill from two well-separated places. Astronomers measure the distance to a star using much the same method.

German astronomer Friedrich Bessel (1784-1846) used this instrument to measure the distance to a star, called 61 Cygni in 1838. The telescope allows two stars to be viewed at the same time and their relative position to be determined accurately.

❑ If the Sun was the size of a basket ball, then the nearest star, called Proxima Centauri, would be 5,350 miles (8,600km) away. If the basket-ball-sized Sun was in San Francisco, Proxima Centauri would be in London. On this scale, only six other stars could be fitted into the sphere of the Earth.

❑ The distance that light travels in one year is called a light-year. 1 light-year = 5.9 million million miles = 9.46 million million km.

❑ Barnard's star is approaching the Sun at a speed of 87 miles/sec (140km/sec). By the year 11,800, it will be the closest star to us.

❑ If you traveled to Proxima Centauri, the star nearest to Earth, the Sun would appear to you to be a bright star in the constellation of Cassiopeia.

❑ A car traveling at a constant speed of 60mph (100km/h) would take over 48 million years to reach the nearest star, Proxima Centauri. This is about 685,000 average human lifetimes.

❑ In October 1991, astronomers at Cambridge, England, discovered one of the dimmest stars ever seen. It is relatively close to Earth, but so dim – 10,000 times fainter than the Sun – that it is visible only with a large telescope.

Winking stars

Many stars vary in brightness. A good example is the star Algol, which is found in the constellation of Perseus. Every 2 days, 20 hours, 48 minutes and 56 seconds, Algol rapidly fades to less than half its normal brightness. It stays dim for about ten hours then, just as rapidly as it faded, Algol grows bright again. The reason for Algol's strange behavior is that it is not one star, but actually two stars, one bright and one dim. The two stars are orbiting around one another. When the dim star moves in front of the bright star, some light from the bright star is blocked from view – Algol becomes fainter. After a short time, the dim star moves from in front of the bright star – Algol regains its normal brightness. Pairs of stars that behave in this way are called eclipsing binaries. Another kind of winking star is the 'Cepheid variable.' These stars get their name from the constellation of Cepheus. Delta Cephei, the fourth brightest star in Cepheus, winks every 5.37 days. In this case, the explanation is that the star is pulsating in and out, like a balloon being blown up and then deflated. When the star is smallest, it is bright. When the star expands, it grows dimmer. So, the star 'winks' as it pulsates. Cepheid variables are very useful stars to astronomers because by watching how quickly such a star winks, and measuring its brightness, it is possible to calculate how far away the star is. Cepheid variables are important 'distance indicators' for astronomers to work with.

Color-enhanced image of a triple star system called Beta Monocerotis, in the constellation of the Unicorn. The system comprises a close double star with a third attendant star.

This sequence of images shows the eclipse of a binary star as a dim companion star passes in front of it. Whereas the surrounding stars remain unchanged, the star near the center disappears completely from view for a period of about five minutes.

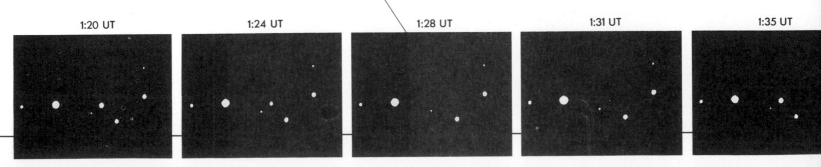

| 1:20 UT | 1:24 UT | 1:28 UT | 1:31 UT | 1:35 UT |

An eclipsing binary star consists of a faint star circling a larger bright star. When the faint star passes in front of the bright star, the brightness of the pair drops sharply. When the faint star goes behind the bright star, there is a small drop in brightness. The graph shows these dips in brightness.

The flashing light of an ambulance is the mechanical equivalent of an eclipsing binary star. A metal baffle rotates around the bulb, blocking the beam as it turns.

The constellation of Auriga, the Charioteer. The bright star is called Capella. It is the sixth brightest star in the sky. To the right of Capella is Epsilon Aurigae, a famous eclipsing binary star.

❑ Polaris, the Pole Star, is a variable star. Its brightness varies, dimming slightly every 4 days, then the star grows bright again. It is at least 7,000 times more luminous than the Sun, and is 680 light-years away.

❑ Plaskett's star, lying about 2,700 light-years away in the constellation of Monoceros, is really two stars circling one another every 14 days. The largest of the stars is 55 times heavier than the Sun.

❑ The star called Epsilon Aurigae is really a binary system: two stars revolving around one another. One of the stars may be the largest known. Its diameter is 2,800 times that of the Sun.

❑ Mizar, the star in the middle of the handle of Ursa Major – the Big Dipper, or Plough – is a double star. With the unaided eye, it is possible to see a companion star, called Alcor, near Mizar.

❑ Mira, the Wonderful star, is found in the constellation of Cetus, the whale or sea monster, right in the middle of the monster's neck. Mira is a large star, three times larger than the Earth's orbit, even at its smallest. But every 11 months, it swells up to twice its volume. Its brightness also varies enormously. At some times it is 1,500 times brighter than at others.

Nebulae – space gas

The space between the stars is not as empty as might at first be thought. It contains much gas and dust. Some of this can be seen as faint, glowing clouds, called nebulae. The nebulae visible in the sword of Orion, and the Crab nebula in Taurus, are well-known examples. Space gas is mainly made up of hydrogen. Much of the gas is dark and invisible against the night sky, except where it lies in front of a bright part of the sky. Here the gas blots out light coming toward us from distant stars, and forms a dark 'hole' in the sky. The Coal Sack, in southern skies near the Southern Cross, is such a dark nebula. Many nebulae however, glow brightly, lit by the stars within the dust cloud. The stars give out ultraviolet radiation and X-rays. This radiation is absorbed by the hydrogen gas in the nebula, and as a result the gas glows. The process is exactly the same as in a neon sign. Inside the sign neon gas is made to glow by supplying electrical energy. In a nebula, the energy is not supplied in the form of electricity but as ultraviolet radiation. The effect is the same – glowing gas. As well as visible light, nebulae also emit infrared and ultraviolet radiation, X-rays, and gamma rays.

Artificially-colored picture of the Dumbell nebula. The Dumbell is a 'planetary' nebula, consisting of a expanding ring of gas ejected from a star about 50,000 years ago.

Part of the Milky Way, showing the North America nebula (lower right), whose shape resembles the North American continent. The nebula lies about 1,600 light-years from Earth. It was discovered by German astronomer William Herschel in 1786 and named by another German, Max Wolf, in 1890.

Artificially-colored photograph of the Horsehead nebula, a dark nebula, three light-years across, in the constellation of Orion. The dark shape is created by thick dust which absorbs light from the stars beyond.

The Orion nebula, a bright cloud of gas and dust also in the constellation of Orion where stars are forming. The nebula is about 1,600 light-years away from Earth, and 15 light-years across. It can be seen with the naked eye.

The Trifid nebula, in the constellation of Sagittarius, shows dark dust lanes that appear to cut through the red nebula, although they are in fact in the foreground. The red color is caused by glowing hydrogen gas.

❏ Space dust is extremely small – smaller than a particle of smoke – and widely separated, with more than 320ft (100m) between individual particles. Nevertheless, the dust greatly hinders stargazing, because it absorbs light which passes through it.

❏ The Veil nebula was formed by an explosion which took place about 30,000 years ago, when the first people lived on the Earth. The nebula is about 2,500 light-years away from Earth.

❏ Interstellar gas contains many complicated chemicals, such as alcohol. It is estimated that the gas cloud in the Sagittarius constellation contains enough alcohol to fill 10,000 million million million million whisky bottles.

❏ A cup of the air we breathe contains about 1,000 million million million atoms. A cupful of space gas contains as few as 10,000 atoms.

❏ The Tarantula nebula is the largest nebula known. It is 160,000 light-years away. If it was as close to us as the Orion nebula, its light would cast shadows on Earth.

❏ The Tarantula nebula is thought to contain a huge star of over 1,000 times the mass of the Sun, ten times more massive than any star in the Milky Way.

A star is born

An artificially-colored radio view of star formation, produced by the Nobeyama Radio Observatory, Japan. The multicolored areas are protostars – balls of hydrogen gas.

A planetary system forming? A disk of material, viewed edge on (red and yellow), is seen around the star Beta Pictoris, extending 62,000 million miles (100,000 million km) into space.

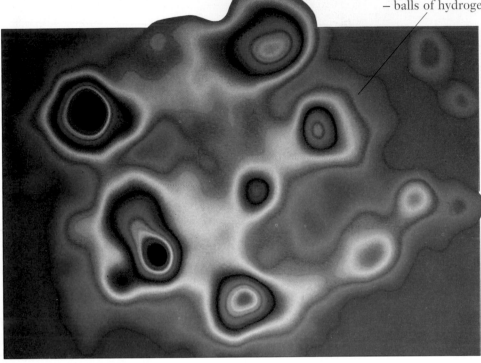

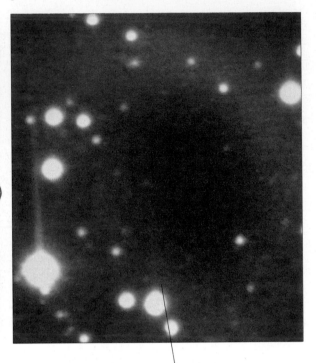

A small dark nebula known as a Bok globule. Bok globules are clouds of gas collapsing to form a star.

An infrared image of a newborn star called Barnard 5 (red patch arrowed) embedded in a cloud of gas and dust.

Stars are born deep inside nebulae and dust clouds in space. The newly created stars can sometimes be seen as dark patches, outlined against the bright background of a nebula. Gravity pulls the thin gas of the nebula into balls of denser gas that block the light from the glowing nebula. Perhaps the process starts when, quite by chance, a swirl of gas forms that is denser than the neighboring gas. The gravity of the dense swirl in turn attracts nearby gas and so a ball of gas forms. The ball shrinks, pulled inward by its own gravity. Inside the shinking gas balls – called protostars – the pressure and temperature rise. This happens because all gases get hotter as they are squeezed into a smaller space. For example, if a bicycle pump is compressed while the exit hole is blocked with a finger, the trapped gas inside becomes hot as its pressure rises. This same process heats up the protostars. Eventually the temperature at the center of the protostar rises to around 18 million °F (10 million °C). This is hot enough to start the nuclear fusion process. Hydrogen – the main material of the protostar – is converted into helium, and in the process energy is released. This energy flows outward as heat and light. The star bursts into life.

❏ The dense globules of gas from which stars are born are much larger than the stars they will form. In the Orion nebula, globules have been detected which are 500 times larger than the Solar System.

❏ An average-sized gas cloud may take several million years to shrink enough to start shining as a star. Very large clouds, about 40 times more massive than the Sun, can start shining in a few thousand years. Once a star starts shining, it can brighten up to full strength quite quickly, in less than a year.

❏ A new star is born in our Galaxy every 18 days. About 20 new stars are born each year. For comparision, there are about 100,000 million stars in our Galaxy.

❏ A brown dwarf is a very small, dark object, with a mass less than one-tenth that of the Sun. They are 'failed stars' — globules of gas that have shrunk under gravity, but have failed to ignite and shine as stars.

Middle-aged stars

A hydrogen bomb explosion at Bikini Atoll on May 21, 1956. The energy of the bomb is produced by nuclear fusion, the process that powers the stars. In nuclear fusion, hydrogen nuclei, made of particles called protons, join together to form a helium nucleus, releasing energy in the process.

If stars are like giant hydrogen bombs, why don't they explode and blow apart? Some stars – called supernovae – do explode, but most stars lead quieter lives. The enormous energy generated by the nuclear reactions within them is balanced by other forces, producing stable, well-behaved stars. The heat at a star's center causes the surrounding gases to expand, moving outward from the center. But the expansion does not go on forever. The gases cool as they expand. Eventually the gases are so cool that the expansion stops. Now gravity takes over, pulling the gases back toward the center. The gas becomes reheated as it falls back towards the center, and so the cycle is repeated. Eventually a state of balance is reached, with the outward pressure of the expanding gas balanced by the inward pull of gravity. The balance is preserved because the amount of energy radiated by the star exactly equals the energy produced inside the star. Stars spend most of their lives in this balanced state. This is the middle age of a star's life. The Sun is a middle-aged star. Eventually, all stars run out of their nuclear fuel. When this happens, the nuclear furnace inside the star stops producing energy, and the star dies.

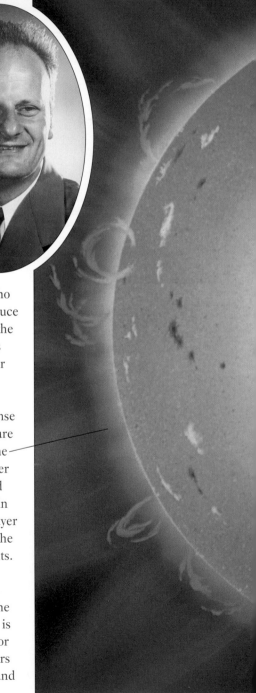

Hans Bethe, the physicist who discovered how the stars produce their energy. He worked on the first atomic bomb, and was awarded the Nobel Prize for Physics in 1967.

In the center of a star is a dense core where fusion reactions are generating energy. Above the core is a relatively stable layer where energy is transferred outward by radiation. This in turn is covered by an active layer where the heat is carried to the surface by convection currents.

The Hertzsprung-Russell diagram, a graph in which the surface temperature of stars is plotted against their power or luminosity. Middle-aged stars fall into a narrow diagonal band called the main sequence.

Hertzsprung-Russell diagram

Luminosity (Sun = 1)

Red supergiants	
Blue giants	
Red giants	
Main sequence	Sun
White dwarfs	
Red dwarfs	

Luminosity values: 10,000 — 100 — 1 — 0.01 — 0.0001

Temperature (°K): 30,000 — 10,000 — 5,000 — 2,500

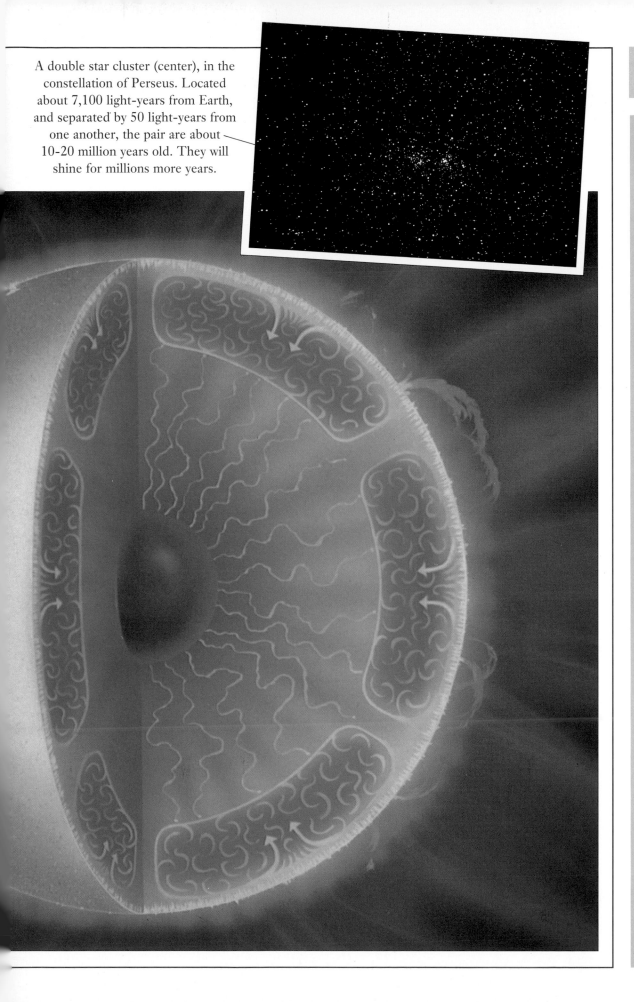

A double star cluster (center), in the constellation of Perseus. Located about 7,100 light-years from Earth, and separated by 50 light-years from one another, the pair are about 10-20 million years old. They will shine for millions more years.

❏ Inside a star, the temperature can reach 29 million °F (16 million °C). The heat radiating from a pin heated to this temperature on Earth would kill everything within 100 miles (160km) of it.

❏ For every kilogram of hydrogen consumed during nuclear fusion in a star, enough energy is produced to keep 30 million electricity-generating power stations operating for a year.

❏ The color of a star shows how hot it is. The coldest stars, with temperatures of about 5,000°F (2,800°C) are red. Hotter stars are yellow or white. The hottest stars, with temperatures of over 60,000°F (33,000°C), are blue.

❏ The Sun will spend 10,000 million years in total as a well-behaved 'middle-aged' star. The heaviest stars age much more quickly and survive for about 10 million years. Lightweight stars can last for 1,000,000 million years.

❏ Hans Bethe, a German astronomer working in America, discovered how stars generate their power by the process of nuclear fusion. during a train trip. In 1938, returning from a conference to Cornell University, New York, Bethe started to jot down some ideas on the back of an envelope. By the time the train reached its destination, Bethe had mapped out the main features of the theory.

Red giants

No star lives forever. When a star has consumed all its nuclear fuel, it dies. Stars, however, do not just flicker and go out, as a candle does when it is extinguished. Exactly what happens when a star runs out of fuel depends upon the mass of the star. Massive stars die in a different way from smaller stars. An average-mass star, like the Sun, swells up and gets hotter as it runs out of fuel. It becomes a giant, bloated star – a red giant. This transformation is brought about by changes deep inside the star. Here, the hydrogen fuel is burnt to produce helium. The helium, which is heavier than hydrogen, falls to the center of the star, forming a helium core. This core does not burn, but its gravity attracts the hydrogen that is burning around it. The hydrogen is squeezed into a smaller space, and as a result becomes hotter still, and burns more fiercely. The extra heat produced makes the star swell up. Toward the end of its life, about 5,000 million years from now, the Sun will gradually grow larger until it is 100 times bigger and 500 times brighter than it is today. It will become a red giant. The bloated Sun will engulf the inner planets, and raise daytime temperatures on Earth to 2,600°F (1,425°C). The Earth's atmosphere and oceans will evaporate. The surface rocks will melt. Life on Earth will cease.

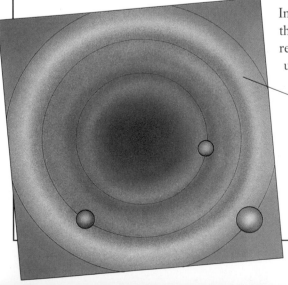

In 5,000 million years, the Sun will become a red giant, and swallow up the inner planets. Mercury and Venus will be engulfed. The Earth may not be destroyed, but it will certainly become a red-hot ball of rock. All life will have been destroyed.

Artist's impression of a planet's death. A tiny blue-white star, seen just above the planet's horizon, orbits a red giant star. The roasted surface of the planet is all that remains of a once-pleasant land. But as one world dies, another takes its place. At center right is a great, pink nebula where new stars and planets are in the making.

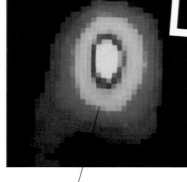

A computer-enhanced image showing a halo of gas around Betelgeuse, the bright red giant star which forms the shoulder (top left as seen from the northern hemisphere) of Orion.

An infrared image of the supergiant star R Coronae Borealis taken by the IRAS infrared observatory satellite. The colors indicate the density of tiny dust particles around the star. It can be found in the bowl of the crown of the Corona Borealis, the Northern Crown, a constellation adjoining Boötes.

Bright stars in the sky at twilight. At the center is the red giant Betelgeuse, in the constellation of Orion. The bright star toward the bottom left is Sirius, the Dog Star, which is the brightest star in the sky. The star directly above it, near the top edge, is Procyon.

FACT FILE

❏ The giant red star Betelgeuse – the red star in the shoulder of the constellation of Orion – is 700 million miles (1,100 million km) across, about 800 times larger than the Sun. Light takes 1 hour to travel from one side of the giant star to the other.

❏ A red giant star like Mira, in the constellation of the Whale, is large enough to swallow up 100 million Suns, yet it contains no more matter than the Sun. It is not much denser than the best 'vacuum' that can be created in a laboratory here on Earth.

❏ If a red giant star was the size of an ordinary living room, its energy-generating core would be the size of the period at the end of this sentence.

❏ If we imagine that the total lifetime of the Sun is 100 years, then it is now about halfway through its life, and is aged 46 years. When the Sun is 85, it will swell into a red giant. At age 99, the Sun will grow so large that it will probably engulf the Earth.

❏ The Earth receives as much heat from the orange star Arcturus, the brightest star in the Herdsman constellation, as we would feel from a candle placed 5 miles (8km) away.

❏ The most luminous star is probably Eta Carinae, which has a maximum luminosity of around 5,000,000 times that of the Sun.

White dwarfs

A red giant star has trouble holding on to its bloated outer layers. They are only loosely attached to the star, and easily float away into space. The slightest disturbance is likely to make the outer gas layers wobble, like a blancmange or jelly. Such stars can even start to pulsate, growing and shrinking in a regular way. This unstable behavior becomes more frequent as a red giant uses up the last dregs of its fuel. Sometimes a 'smoke ring' of material is formed around the star as the outer layers waft gently into space. The ring, called a planetary nebula, moves outward from the star. At the center of the ring, a small dim star is sometimes seen – a white dwarf. A white dwarf is the remains of a red giant that has run out of fuel. It is made up of the 'cinders' remaining after the star's nuclear furnace has gone out. These cinders consist of the parts of atoms – electrons and nuclei – squeezed together very tightly by gravity. This material is very dense, about 100,000 times as dense as water. A piece of a white dwarf which is merely the size of a sugar cube weighs around 2,200lb (1 tonne).

Computer-colored view of Sirius, the brightest star in the sky. The star has a dim white dwarf companion, Sirius B, which was the first white dwarf to be discovered.

Artist's impression of a white dwarf star formed after a red giant has run out of nuclear fuel and cast off its outer layers. The small dim star throws little light or heat on the frozen planet orbiting it.

Menkar, a red giant in the constellation Cetus
D: 48,000,000 miles

Rigel, the seventh brightest star in the sky
D: 26,000,000 miles

Arcturus, the brightest
star in Boötes
D: 17,000,000 miles

Capella   D: 4,000,000 miles

Eta Aurigae   D: 3,000,000 miles

Sirius A   D: 1,700,000 miles

The Sun   D: 865,000 miles

Proxima Centauri   D: 216,000 miles

Sirius B, a white dwarf   D: 32,000 miles

The Earth   D: 7,927 miles

A white dwarf, about five times the size of the Earth, is indeed a dwarf beside the supergiant Alpha Aquarii. Menkar, Rigel, Arcturus, Eta Aurigae, and Capella qualify as giants as they are much larger than the smaller main sequence stars shown. The basic color of a star is an indication of its temperature. Blue stars are the hottest. Cooler stars are white, yellow, orange, or red.

Sirius, also called the Dog Star, shines brightly in the constellation of the Great Dog, Canis Major.

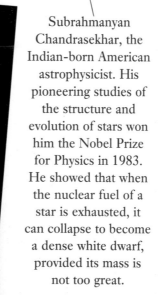

Subrahmanyan Chandrasekhar, the Indian-born American astrophysicist. His pioneering studies of the structure and evolution of stars won him the Nobel Prize for Physics in 1983. He showed that when the nuclear fuel of a star is exhausted, it can collapse to become a dense white dwarf, provided its mass is not too great.

New stars for old

On the night of June 8, 1918, a new star appeared in the constellation of Aquila, the Eagle. Within a few hours the star became as bright as Sirius, the brightest star in the sky. By the next day, however, the star had begun to fade. After a few weeks, it was invisible to the naked eye. Stars which suddenly become bright for a short time are reasonably common, although the 1918 star was the brightest for 300 years. Such stars are called novae, from the Latin for 'new.' Novae occur in double stars or binary star systems, in which one star orbits around another. For a nova to occur, one star must be a white dwarf and the other a red giant. The loosely-held outer layers of the red giant are attracted by the strong force of gravity exerted by the white dwarf. Hydrogen gas streams from the red giant toward the white dwarf. The gas is heated as it falls on to the surface of the dwarf. Eventually the hydrogen gas becomes so hot that nuclear fusion can start. An uncontrolled nuclear explosion takes place, throwing enough material to make 30 Earths into space at enormous speeds. The flash of the explosion can shine as brightly as 100,000 Suns. After a few days, the energy of the explosion dies down, and the star returns to its normal state.

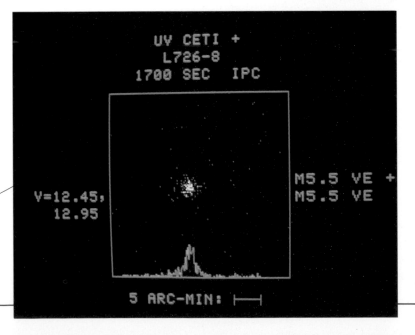

X-ray image of the flare star UV Ceti, taken with the Einstein observatory satellite. Flare stars are seen to brighten suddenly, over a period of a few minutes, and then fade again more slowly. The flares may be giant versions of similar flares seen on the surface of the Sun.

An artificially-colored image of the remnants of Nova Persei, which exploded in 1901. The remnants form a shell of expanding gas ejected in the explosion which is about 0.7 light-years across.

A nova explodes when material from a red giant falls onto the surface of a companion white dwarf. The explosion can make the pair of stars shine a million times more brightly than normal.

Special effects photograph showing the nova explosion of a star, observed by radio telescopes on Earth. Astronomers have seen some novae explode several times.

❏ About 40 novae erupt in our Galaxy each year.

❏ The layer of gas that spreads out from a nova explosion can be traveling at speeds of 5 million mph (8 million km/h).

❏ The most luminous star ever seen is called Eta Carinae. In 1843 it flared up until it was the second brightest star in the sky, even though it is 4,000 light-years from Earth. Its light output was more than 5 million times greater than that of the Sun.

❏ The Blaze Star is a recurrent nova in the constellation of Corona Borealis, the Northern Crown. It usually cannot be seen with the unaided eye but twice, in 1866 and 1946, it has increased in brightness so that it could be seen briefly.

❏ A typical nova explosion releases about as much energy as the Sun emits in 10,000 years, or as much as in 1,000,000,000,000,000,000,000 nuclear bombs.

❏ The star of Bethlehem may have been a nova explosion, although no definite conclusion can be reached. According to Chinese records, a nova appeared in the constellation of Capricornus in March A.D. 5. The traditional date of Jesus' birth – 25 December A.D. 1 – is probably inaccurate and the birth could have been a few years later.

Exploding stars

Very massive stars live life in the fast lane. They form more quickly than less massive stars from the gas clouds of a nebula. They burst into life more quickly as nuclear fusion starts in their extra hot interiors. They use their nuclear fuel more quickly and, when the fuel runs out, they do not gently waft off their outer layers, but blast them away in an enormous explosion called a supernova. A supernova explosion occurs a matter of seconds after a massive star runs out of fuel. The outer layers of the star are no longer supported by the outflowing of energy from the center, and they quickly collapse toward the center. At the supernova's core, the gas is pressed together and the temperature soars to 90,000 million °F (50,000 million °C), thousands of times hotter than the center of the Sun. Like heated gunpowder within an artillery shell, the center of the star explodes. Gases thrown out by the explosion blast outward fast enough to go from Sydney to London in less than a second. Light, heat, X-rays, and neutrinos pour outward. The exploding star suddenly becomes brighter than a 1,000 million Suns. After the explosion, the remains of the exploded star may produce a neutron star or a black hole.

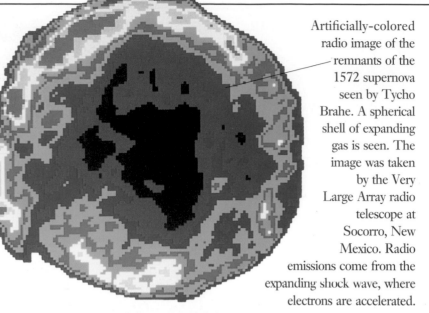

Artificially-colored radio image of the remnants of the 1572 supernova seen by Tycho Brahe. A spherical shell of expanding gas is seen. The image was taken by the Very Large Array radio telescope at Socorro, New Mexico. Radio emissions come from the expanding shock wave, where electrons are accelerated.

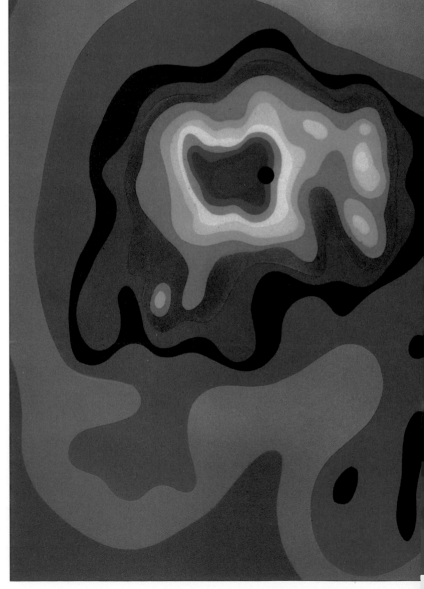

The next supernova? Artificially-colored picture of the star Eta Carinae and its surrounding nebula. The brightness of the star fluctuates wildly. In March 1843 it outshone every star except Sirius. This instability may indicate that the star is about to explode.

Artist's impression of a supernova exploding near a giant orange star. A nearby planet bakes in the intense burst of radiation. On average, one supernova explodes in a galaxy once every 30 years.

Radio image of the Vela supernova remnant recorded by the Parkes radio telescope, Australia. Red indicates the most intense radio emissions, and purple the least intense. The supernova exploded about 11,000 years ago. At the center is a neutron star (black dot).

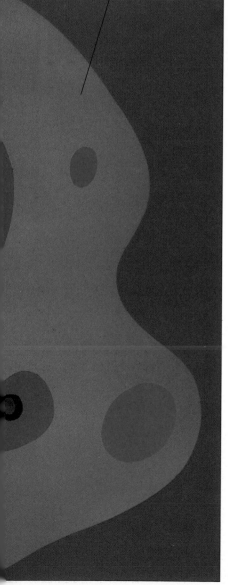

Supernova SN 1987a is the bright 'star' seen here. First observed shining in the Large Magellanic Cloud on February 24, 1987, it was the brightest supernova since 1604, about 250 million times brighter than the Sun.

FACT FILE

❏ When a supernova appeared in A.D. 185, Chinese officials regarded it as a sign of impending revolution. Fearing the worst, the governor of the Yuan-Shou region punished or killed all his middle-ranking officials.

❏ On November 11, 1572, Danish astronomer Tycho Brahe was returning home for supper when he saw a bright supernova in the constellation of Cassiopeia. He recalled the incident, 'directly overhead, a certain strange star was suddenly seen, flashing its light with a radiant gleam. . . . I was led into such perplexity by the unbelievability of the thing that I began to doubt the evidence of my own eyes.' Because of his observations, the star is now known as 'Tycho's Star.'

❏ Other celebrated supernovae have occurred in our Galaxy in the current millennium. In 1006, the brightest supernova seen in our Galaxy, 100 times brighter than Venus, was observed by Chinese astronomers, in the constellation of Lupus. It was visible for 2 years. In 1054, another was seen by Japanese and Chinese astronomers in Taurus. It was visible for 23 days in daylight, and for 21 months at night. The remnants of this explosion make up the Crab Nebula. Another supernova, in 1604, was observed by the German astronomer Johannes Kepler in the constellation of Ophiuchus on October 9.

Cosmic lighthouses

When a massive star dies in a supernova explosion, it leaves behind a 'corpse.' If the star is around three times heavier than the Sun, the corpse is a neutron star, also called a pulsar. A neutron star or pulsar is one of the strangest objects in the Universe. It is not like other stars – a ball of gas that shines because of the nuclear furnace at its center. A neutron star is like a raw egg. It has a hard thin shell with liquid inside. The shell is made of high-strength iron – more than a million times stronger than steel. Inside the star, there is a sea of liquid made up of nuclear particles called neutrons. These neutrons are created when the 'ash' from the supernova is squeezed together by the very strong gravity of the massive exploding star. Neutron stars are small and dense, compared to other stars. The diameter of a neutron star is only about 12 miles (20km), about the size of a town. However, the mass of a neutron star is about the same as the mass of the Sun. This means that the density of neutron star material is 100 million million times that of water. All neutron stars are spinning rapidly. Neutron stars are also called pulsars because they produce very rapid pulses of light, radio waves, and X-rays. These very short and regular pulses are produced as the pulsar spins around. The first pulsar discovered in 1967 sent out a pulse every 1.33730 seconds. Some pulsars are so regular that they can be used as very accurate clocks, only losing a second in a million years.

The first pulsar was discovered in November 1967 at the Mullard Radio Astronomy Observatory at Cambridge University, England, by Antony Hewish and Jocelyn Bell-Burnell (above, photographed in 1977).

Artificially-colored image of the Crab nebula, a supernova remnant in the constellation of Taurus. At its center is the Crab pulsar, a rapidly spinning neutron star which is the tiny, dense remains of the star which exploded.

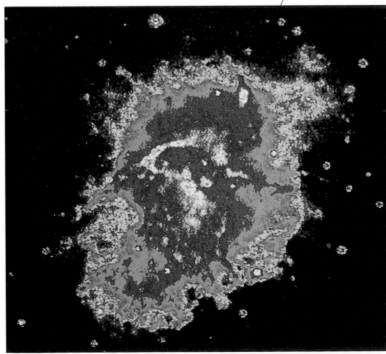

Artificially-colored image of the Vela pulsar (pink and blue, upper right), a neutron star which is spinning 13 times a second, emitting pulses of light and radio waves.

X-ray image of the Vela supernova remnant and pulsar, 1,600 light-years from Earth. The pulsar emits a pulse of radio waves every 0.089 seconds.

A sequence of views of the Vela pulsar (a faint object just left of center) flashing (first and third frames of bottom row).

❏ A teaspoonful of neutron star material weighs about 110 million tons (100 million tonnes).

❏ Some neutron stars spin 600 times a second, which is as fast as a dentist's drill. The surface temperature of a neutron star is about 1.8 million °F (1 million °C).

❏ The force of gravity is very strong on a neutron star because of its amazing density. Your weight on a neutron star would be 10,000 million times greater than on Earth.

❏ If an astronaut tried to land on a neutron star, he or she would be crushed by the extremely strong force of gravity, and squashed into a thin layer less than one atom thick.

❏ A neutron star is the strongest magnet in the Universe. The magnetic field of a neutron star is a million million times stronger than the Earth's magnetism.

❏ Our Galaxy probably contains millions of old neutron stars that have stopped spinning, and so are undetectable.

❏ When the first pulsar signal was detected in 1967, it was thought that its signals might be a message from an alien civilization deep in space. The signal was jokingly labelled 'LGM,' for 'little green men.'

The ultimate trash can

When a very massive star (more than 30 times the mass of the Sun) explodes, the stellar remnant may form a black hole. A black hole comes into being when the gravity of the exploding star is so strong that it squeezes the 'ash' of the explosion completely out of existence. It is as if there was a hole in space, into which the ash has vanished. In fact, anything falling into the hole will never be seen again. Even light cannot escape. A black hole is the ultimate trash can; nothing thrown in ever comes back! Has a black hole ever been detected? Looking for a black hole is rather like looking for a black cat in a coal cellar at night. Because black holes give out no light, there is little to reveal their presence. However, in some circumstances, black holes may give themselves away. If an ordinary star is close to a black hole, the intense gravity of the black hole may drag gas away from the star. The gas gets hotter and hotter as it falls toward the black hole. Just before disappearing into the hole, the gas releases a burst of X-rays. So, strong X-ray sources may be black holes. The best candidate so far identified seems to be a star in the constellation of Cygnus. This star seems to have an invisible companion that weighs as much as 10 Suns, and which gives out X-rays, as predicted.

Looking toward the center of our Galaxy, in the constellation of Sagittarius. A black hole, weighing millions of times more than the Sun, may lie hidden behind the stars and dust.

Material being drawn from the surface of a star into a black hole. Blue lines represent gravity.

Artist's impression of a stream of gas being pulled from the atmosphere of red giant (upper left) by the immense gravity of a black hole (upper right).

The Centaurus A galaxy. The galaxy's most distinctive feature is the great lane of dust (shown purple) which bisects it. Located 16 million light-years away, Centaurus A is thought to have a black hole at its core.

Artist's impression of the galaxy M87 as it might appear from a nearby planet. M87 is a giant galaxy, believed to have a black hole, with the mass of 5,000 million Suns, situated near its center.

❏ A possible black hole is the X-ray star LMC X-3 in the Large Magellanic Cloud. LMC X-3 is about ten times heavier than the Sun, but only measures about 3½ miles (6km) across.

❏ There may be a giant black hole at the center of our Galaxy, weighing as much as four million Suns. The black hole may be capturing stars, gas, and dust equivalent to the weight of three Earths every year.

❏ The Sun would have to collapse to a radius of 1.8 miles (3km) to form a black hole. The Earth would have to be squeezed into a radius of one-third of an inch (9mm) to be dense enough to form a black hole.

❏ Near a medium-sized black hole, the stretching force of the intense gravity field would be the same as if you were hanging from a bridge with the the entire population of New York or London dangling from your ankles.

❏ In April 1991, scientists discovered a galaxy, known as NGC 6240, which may contain a black hole 100,000 million times as massive as the Sun. The black hole is as massive as the whole Milky Way, but its diameter is only one-thirtieth that of the Milky Way.

❏ Time slows down near a black hole; inside a black hole it stops completely.

Star clusters

One of the most beautiful sights in the night sky is the Pleiades or Seven Sisters cluster of stars. It seems to the unaided eye to contain only seven stars, but it may actually contain 500 stars altogether. The Pleiades stars are about 20 million years old, young by astronomical standards. The young blue-white stars are surrounded by wisps of gas and dust in which stars are still forming. Much older, but an equally beautiful sight, are the 'globular' clusters that are spread around our Galaxy. A globular cluster is a group of about a million stars, crammed into a spherical space only 60 light-years across. The stars at the center of a globular cluster are close together. If the Earth was at the center of such a cluster, the night sky would be packed with bright stars. You would even be able to see your shadow by their light. Globular clusters are the oldest objects in the Galaxy, formed before the stars in the disk of the Galaxy, some 13,000 million years ago. By studying the apparent brightness and color of the stars in a globular cluster, it is possible to calculate the distance of the cluster. Because of this, globular clusters have become an important means of estimating distances to far-off galaxies.

Artificially-colored image of M13, a great globular star cluster in the constellation of Hercules. The cluster, first identified by Edmond Halley, is the largest globular cluster in the northern sky.

Artificially-colored image of the Pleiades or Seven Sisters cluster of stars, which are situated 410 light-years away in the constellation of Taurus. The brightest stars are all surrounded by streaky bright regions which appears purple in this view. This is caused by cold gas and dust reflecting the light of the young, blue stars nearby.

The Pleiades (top) star cluster. The seven brightest stars are named after Atlas and his daughters. The brightest is called Alcyone. The others are Maia, Atlas, Electra, Merope, Taygete, and Pleione. The fuzzy object at the bottom of the image is Halley's Comet.

The globular star cluster M5 in the constellation of Serpens. Discovered in 1702 by German Gottfried Kirch, it is the second brightest globular cluster in the northern sky. It is located 27,000 light-years away and is about 130 light-years across.

The constellation of Taurus, the Bull. The brightest star, on the bull's right eye is Aldebaran, which is near the Hyades star cluster. The Pleiades cluster can be found on the animal's shoulder.

❏ The Greek poet Hesiod, who lived around 700 B.C., emphasized the role of the Pleiades in planning the seasonal cycle of farm work:

When Atlas-born, the Pleiad stars arise
Before the Sun above the dawning skies,
'Tis time to reap, and when they sink below
The morn-illumined west, 'tis time to sow.

❏ According to ancient Chinese legend, the appearance of the Hyades group of stars in the sky means rain. Interestingly, Roman and Greek legends say the same thing.

❏ The Hercules globular cluster is the brightest globular cluster in the northern hemisphere sky. It was discovered by English scientist Edmond Halley in 1714.

❏ In 1974, radio astronomers beamed a message to the globular cluster M13 but, as the signal will take 22,500 years to reach its destination, no reply can be expected until around 47,000 A.D.

❏ There are only four globular clusters that can be seen with the naked eye. Two lie in the northern sky: M5 in Serpens and M13 in Hercules, which is always visible from North America and Europe. Two are in the southern sky: Omega Centauri, the brightest globular cluster, and 47 Tucanae, near the Small Magellanic Cloud.

Galaxies – star cities

The largest clusters of stars, dust, and gas are called galaxies. To the unaided eye, galaxies look like faint blurs in the night sky, but a telescope reveals that they are made up of thousands of millions of stars. A typical galaxy contains 100,000 million stars, and may be 100,000 light-years across. There are between 100,000 and 1,000,000 million galaxies in the Universe. These galaxies are spread thinly throughout the Universe. If a galaxy was the size of a person, galaxies would typically be as close to one another as the players on a large baseball field. We may think of a galaxy as a city of stars, far away from its neighbors. Galaxy City is a big place. If stars in Galaxy City were the size of people, then each star would be 62,000 miles (100,000km) away from its neighbor. The city would spread over an area millions of times larger than Africa. Most galaxies are spiral-shaped. They have a central region, or nucleus, containing many stars. Surrounding this is a flat disk, in which spiral lines of stars can be seen, like the streets of a city leading into the town center. Other galaxies are more uniform in appearance. These are egg-shaped elliptical galaxies. Finally, there are the irregular galaxies with no distinctive shape.

The Sombrero galaxy, a spiral galaxy in the constellation of Virgo. The galaxy is seen almost edge-on and the dark stripe running across it is due to dust lying in the plane of the galaxy. It has a large central bulge.

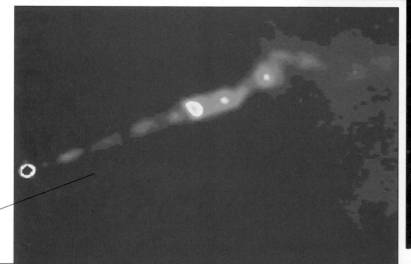

The galaxy M87 in Virgo is emitting a bright jet of gases that shoots a distance of 4,000 light-years into space. At some points, the jet is brighter than 400 million Suns.

Artificially-colored radio image of the barred spiral galaxy NGC 1300 taken by the Very Large Array radio telescope. Red areas indicate gas moving toward the Earth, blue areas show gas moving away.

The galaxy M81 in the constellation of the Great Bear. The photograph has been treated to highlight the different types of stars. Older stars are shown red while younger stars are shown blue.

X-ray image of the galaxy Centaurus A and the jet of matter that flows from it. The galaxy is the larger white spot at the center of the image. It is a strong X-ray source.

Spirals in the sky

Spiral galaxies vary in size, ranging from giants such as the Andromeda galaxy to dwarfs that are only one-tenth as big. Spiral galaxies also vary in their shape; some have three, four, or more arms, others have only two. However, there are some common features. All spiral galaxies have a dense central spherical core of stars, and a thin plate-like disk of stars and dust that surrounds the core, with arms made up of close-packed stars. The disk of the galaxy has a thickness of about one-hundredth of its diameter. A model of a galaxy could be made using a audio record to represent the disk. A table tennis ball would represent the central core at this scale. The stars in the core are old – at least 10,000 million years old, dating from early in the galaxy's life. The stars in the disk are much younger – only a few million years old. In fact, the disk is a star nursery, with stars continually being born from the plentiful dust found there. The stars in the disk orbit around the center of the galaxy, perhaps a hundred times before they die. At certain stages in their orbits, fast-moving stars temporarily pack together to form a bright spiral arm. It is as if the stars were automobiles speeding along a highway, only to encounter a slow-moving lorry. The motorcars pack together behind the slow-moving lorry, just as stars pack together into a slow-moving spiral arm.

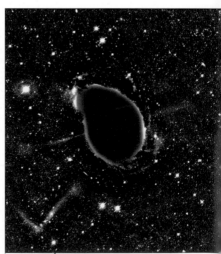

X-ray mosaic of the Andromeda galaxy M31, taken by the Einstein X-ray observatory satellite. The large bright area is the center of the galaxy. In the outer regions, many of the X-ray sources (bright spots) are situated in globular clusters.

Artificially-colored radio image of the spiral galaxy M83 in the Hydra constellation showing the regions of strong magnetic fields (white, violet, red, and yellow).

Artificially-colored image of the spiral galaxy NGC 1232. The central nucleus holds about 1,000 million ancient stars. The spiral arms contain younger stars formed from the plentiful gas found there.

Computer-enhanced photograph of the peculiar spiral galaxy NGC 1097. A feature of the galaxy is the jets of material that flow from it. The central part of the picture has been 'burnt out' in order to make the faint jets visible.

❏ The Andromeda spiral galaxy contains several hundred thousands of millions of stars, and its mass is at least one hundred thousand million times the mass of the Sun.

❏ Stars travel around the center of a galaxy in orbits. In the Milky Way, stars near the center complete one orbit in 10 million years. Further out, our Sun takes about 225 million years to complete an orbit. This period is known as a 'cosmic year.'

❏ Three-quarters of the galaxies in the Universe are spiral galaxies. There are three other types of galaxies: elliptical, irregular, and lenticular (which appear lens-shaped when seen edge-on).

❏ A cloud of globular clusters surrounds both the core and disk of a spiral galaxy. The clusters orbit around the galaxy center, passing through the disk two times each orbit — about once every million years. Both cluster and disk stars are widely separated so there are no collisions between stars.

❏ The spiral arms of a galaxy do not form in the same way as the spirals of cream in a stirred coffee cup. Galaxies are so old that the pattern would have long since vanished if this were the case, just as stirred cream quickly mixes with the coffee.

The Andromeda galaxy can be located in the sky by first finding the Great Square of Pegasus. Cassiopeia makes a good pointer to Pegasus.

Artificially-colored image of the Andromeda galaxy, M31, and its two dwarf satellite galaxies. One is seen top right and the other on the lower edge of the main galaxy.

Our Galaxy

The Milky Way is a river of light through the night sky. It features in the myths of all ancient people. The ancient Greeks, for instance, thought that the Milky Way was formed of milk from the breast of the goddess Hera as she fed the baby Hercules. We get our word 'galaxy' from the Greek word for milk, 'gala.' A telescope reveals that the Milky Way is made up of numerous stars, too numerous to be counted in one brief human lifetime. The Milky Way is a galaxy; it is the galaxy we live in. To mark its special status, we give it a capital letter and call it the Galaxy, or our Galaxy. Our Galaxy is a flat, spiral galaxy. It is slightly larger than the average galaxy, being about 100,000 light-years across. There are at least 100,000 million stars in our Galaxy. About 40,000 million stars are concentrated in the central bulge of the Galaxy around which are wrapped four spiral arms. The Sun lies in one of the arms of the Milky Way, about one-third of the way in from the outer edge. It is about 33,000 light-years from the center. A supersonic airliner such as Concorde would take 17,000 million years to reach the center of the Milky Way flying from Earth at its usual cruising speed. However, it is small compared to some radio galaxies at the edge of the Universe.

Computer-processed radio map of the sky as seen from Earth. The most intense emissions are shown in red.

Artificially-colored image of X-rays coming from the center of our Galaxy produced by the ROSAT satellite. Violet indicates the lowest X-ray intensity, and red the highest.

Artist's impression of our Galaxy. Our Sun is located in the short spur that joins the spiral arm, called the Perseus Arm, at the far right. The Sun orbits at 160 miles per second.

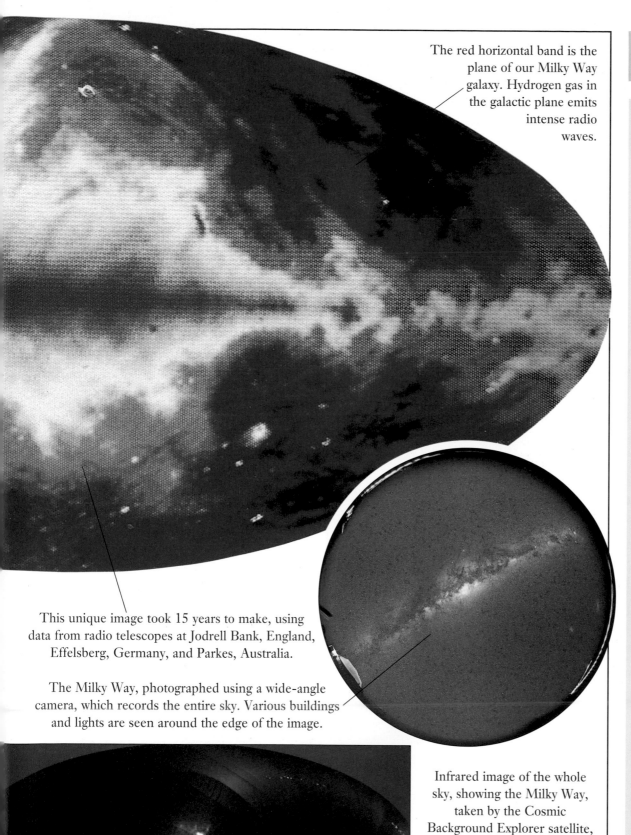

The red horizontal band is the plane of our Milky Way galaxy. Hydrogen gas in the galactic plane emits intense radio waves.

This unique image took 15 years to make, using data from radio telescopes at Jodrell Bank, England, Effelsberg, Germany, and Parkes, Australia.

The Milky Way, photographed using a wide-angle camera, which records the entire sky. Various buildings and lights are seen around the edge of the image.

Infrared image of the whole sky, showing the Milky Way, taken by the Cosmic Background Explorer satellite, launched November 18, 1989. The infrared sky is dominated by radiation from cold dust which lies between the stars in our Galaxy (bright horizontal band).

The Milky Way's neighborhood

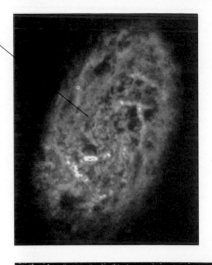

Radio image of the Triangulum galaxy M33, a member of the Local Group of galaxies. Located 2.4 million light-years away, it has a diameter of 40,000 light-years and a mass of 15,000 million Suns.

Our Galaxy, the Milky Way, is not alone in our local part of space. There are about ten small galaxies close by. If we think of our Galaxy as a city, then these galaxies are small outlying villages close to Milky Way city. The largest of the neighboring galaxies are the Large Magellanic Cloud, and the Small Magellanic Cloud. The Large Magellanic Cloud is about 160,000 light-years away – close by astronomical standards. It is a quarter the size of the Milky Way. The Small Magellanic Cloud is about 185,000 light-years away. The Magellanic Clouds are irregular galaxies – they have no regular shape. There are other irregular galaxies nearby – one is less than one-sixth the size of the Small Magellanic Cloud, and another is one-tenth the size. The other nearby galaxies are small spiral or elliptical galaxies. The nearest large galaxy – the nearest large star city – is the Andromeda spiral galaxy. This is about ten times further from the Milky Way than the Magellanic Clouds. Andromeda is larger than the Milky Way, about 160,000 light-years across. Like the Milky Way, Andromeda is surrounded by smaller galaxies – star villages – of spiral or elliptical shape. The whole collection of nearby galaxies is called the Local Group of galaxies. There are about 20 galaxies in the Local Group. If galaxies are cities or villages, the Local Group corresponds to a county.

The major members of the Local Group of galaxies to which our Milky Way belongs. It also contains the Andromeda galaxy, the Large and Small Magellanic Clouds, and various dwarf galaxies. The Andromeda galaxy is 1.5 times the size of our Galaxy and 2.2 million light-years away. Our Galaxy is the second largest in the Local Group, followed in size by the Triangulum spiral which is about half the size of the Milky Way and 2.4 million light-years away. The Large Magellanic Cloud is a quarter the size of the Milky Way, and the Small Cloud one-sixth of the size.

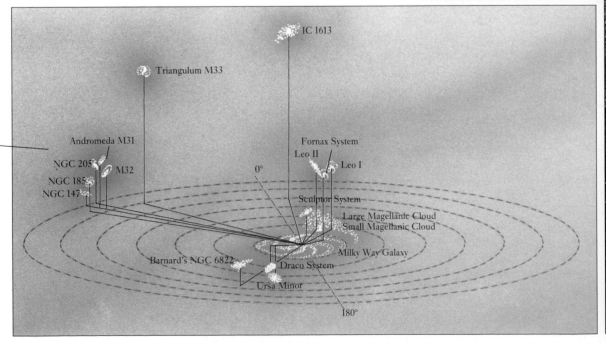

The Tarantula nebula, an enormous bright cloud of glowing gas which lies within the Large Magellanic Cloud. The nebula is so bright that, were it as close as the Orion nebula, it would be visible during the day.

The Large Magellanic Cloud, one of two irregular, dwarf galaxies which orbit our own Galaxy, the Milky Way. The pinkish patch at the left is the Tarantula Nebula.

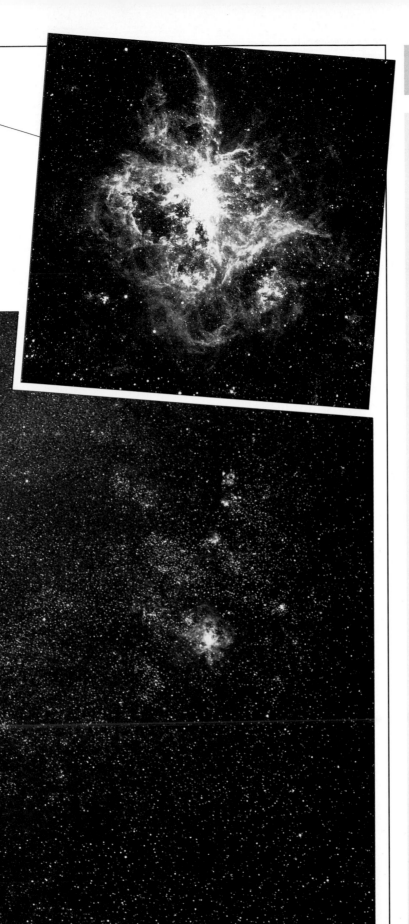

❏ The Andromeda galaxy (seen above) is the largest member of our Local Group of galaxies. The Milky Way is second largest in this group.

❏ The Local Group of galaxies is moving through space at a speed of 1,343,000mph (2,160,000km/h).

❏ The two brightest galaxies visible in the night sky (apart from the Milky Way, of course) are the Magellanic Clouds that can be seen with the unaided eye. They look like detached parts of the Milky Way but cannot be seen from North American or European latitudes, north of New Orleans or Cairo.

❏ The Magellanic Clouds are named after the 16th century Portuguese explorer Ferdinand Magellan, who almost became the first person to sail around the world. Unfortunately, Magellan was killed on the journey, but his crew made it back to Spain in 1522.

Clusters of galaxies

Galaxies are rarely alone. They occur in groups of two, three, or more; our Local Group is an example. Sometimes groups of galaxies contain hundreds or thousands of members. These large groups of galaxies are called clusters. The nearest cluster to the Local Group is in the constellation of Virgo. The Virgo cluster contains galaxies of every type: some spiral, some elliptical and some irregular. The cluster lies around 72 million light-years away. Over 2,500 galaxies are packed into the core of the Virgo cluster, a volume not much larger than the Local Group that only contains 20 galaxies. The next nearest cluster lies about 390 million light-years away in the constellation of Coma Berenices. It is a spherical-shaped cluster of about 1,000 members. Although there are many galaxy clusters in the Universe, they are not evenly spaced. Many are grouped into even larger groups called 'super clusters.' The Local Group, for example, is part of a larger group containing both the Virgo cluster and the Coma cluster. If galaxies are cities, and galaxy clusters are counties, then super clusters are states. There is some evidence that super clusters form even larger 'super super clusters.' These would be the continents of the Universe.

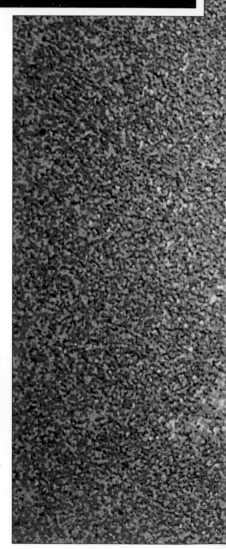

The Virgo cluster of galaxies, the center of our local supercluster. The two bright elliptical galaxies seen in this image are M86 (just above and to the left of center) and M84 (far right).

An X-ray (blue) and radio (red) image of the Virgo cluster of galaxies. The strong X-ray source at the center is the M87 galaxy.

Stephan's Quartet of galaxies, which were discovered in 1877. The galaxy at the lower left is not part of the group as it is much closer to Earth.

The Pavo 5 cluster of galaxies. Pavo, the Peacock, is a constellation in the southern hemisphere. The picture was processed to bring out the faint halos of gas (blue) that surround and link the galaxies (pink).

Computer-processed image of the M87 galaxy, a member of the Virgo cluster. A bright jet of outflowing gas extends from the galaxy center toward the right of the image.

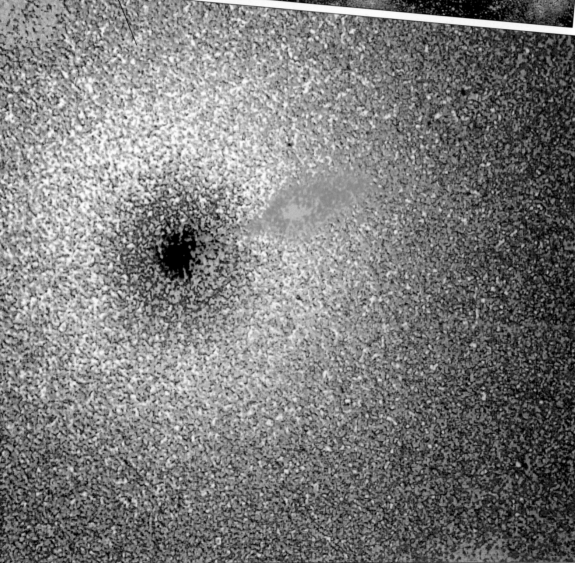

The distant galaxies

Edwin Hubble (1889-1953). In 1923, he measured the distance to the Andromeda galaxy. This led him to confirm that the distant galaxies were moving away from us. Hubble's law states that the recession speed of a galaxy is directly proportional to its distance from us.

In 1914, an American astronomer, Vesto Slipher, made an important discovery. He found that the distant galaxies are moving away from the Earth at very high speed. Slipher's discovery was made by carefully examining the spectrum – the pattern of colors – of the light emitted by the distant galaxies. If a galaxy is receding from the Earth, the light waves from the stars are stretched and the light becomes redder. This effect is called the redshift, and can be used as a kind of stellar speedometer. The greater the redshift, the faster the galaxy is moving away. American astronomer Edwin Hubble heard about Slipher's discovery and decided to investigate further. In 1929, he confirmed Slipher's hypothesis. The distant galaxies were all moving away from the Earth. It is as if the whole Universe is expanding. Imagine a balloon with dots drawn on its surface to represent the galaxies. As the balloon is inflated, it expands and the dots move apart, just as the galaxies are doing.

A distant galaxy, IC4296. The galaxy is 100 million light-years away from Earth and is receding at a speed of 1,600 miles/sec (2,500km/sec). It has two jets of hot gas flowing outward from its center. The ends of the jets are the strong sources of radio waves.

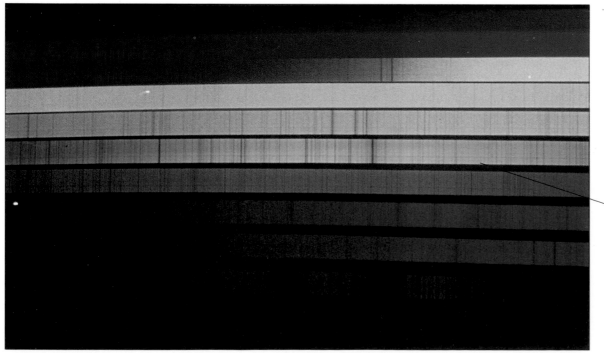

Stephan's Quartet of galaxies and galaxy NGC 7320 (center right). This image has been color-coded to indicate the redshift values of the galaxies. Red indicates a high redshift (i.e. the galaxies are receding at high velocity from us), and blue indicates a low redshift.

The spectrum of the Sun. The dark lines are formed when white light from the Sun's hot interior passes through its cooler outer layers. Certain colors are absorbed by the cooler gas. If a star is receding, the lines in its spectrum are shifted toward the red end of the spectrum – it is redshifted.

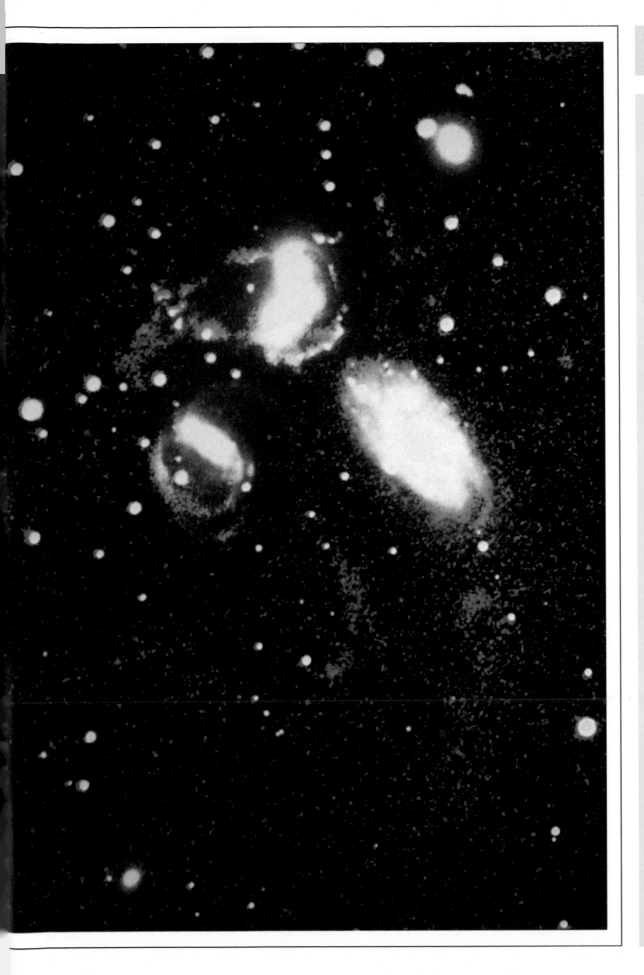

❏ The further away a galaxy is from us, the faster it is traveling away or receding from us. A galaxy has a speed of 47 miles/sec (75km/sec) if it is 3 million light-years away. A galaxy twice this distance away recedes at twice the speed, one three times more distant recedes three time faster, and so on. This is called Hubble's Law, after the great American astronomer, Edwin Hubble.

❏ If a galaxy is moving toward us, its light waves are compressed and appear bluer – this is called the blue shift. Only three galaxies have blue shifts, indicating that they are moving toward us: the two Magellanic Clouds, and the Fornax System. All these galaxies are members of the Local Group. All other galaxies show redshifts, and are thus moving away from us.

❏ By measuring the redshift of a galaxy, the distance to the galaxy can be calculated. The greater the redshift, the more distant the galaxy.

❏ The famous German scientist, Albert Einstein could have predicted that the Universe was expanding, but did not actually do so. His Theory of Relativity showed that the Universe should expand, but he could not believe it. So he 'fiddled' his equations to get the answer he expected. Later he called this the 'the greatest mistake of my life.'

Quasars – the most distant objects

The word 'quasar' is short for 'quasi-stellar radio object,' which is a complicated way of describing something that looks like a star, but which gives out radio waves. The first quasars were discovered in the 1960s by radio astronomers. Since then, over 1,500 quasars have been found. It turns out that most quasars give out light rather than radio waves, and so their name is not wholly appropriate. Quasars are the most distant objects known to us, residing at the very edge of the Universe. Like all distant cosmic objects, quasars are moving away from us at great speed, as the Universe expands. Astronomers can only see quasars because they emit huge amounts of energy, as light, radio waves, or X-rays. Quasars are about 1,000 times brighter than a galaxy. For such powerful objects, quasars are amazingly small. A quasar is about 1 light-*day* in diameter, compared with a galaxy that is about 100,000 light-*years* across. Put another way, a quasar is about 36,500,000 times smaller than a galaxy. The best explanation for the power of a quasar suggests that it consists of a large black hole in the center of a galaxy. The black hole swallows up stars and dust from the galaxy, converting the material into energy. This process would produce 1,000 times more energy than the nuclear fusion of hydrogen into helium. The most luminous quasars would need a black hole as massive as 100 million Suns to power them, but this actually only constitutes about 0.1 percent of the mass of the surrounding galaxy.

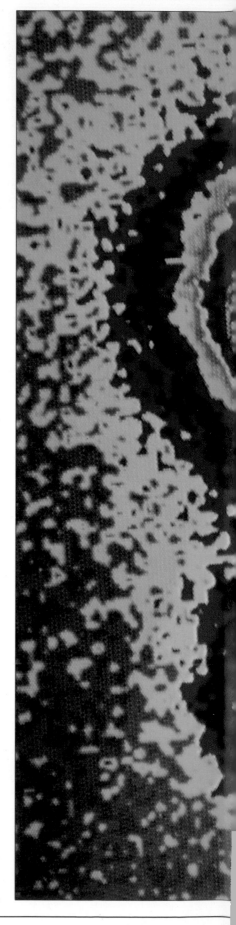

Artificially-colored image of the spiral galaxy NGC 4319 and the quasar Markarian 205 (small circular object at bottom). The quasar appears to be connected to the galaxy by a faint bridge of material. However, observations showed that the two are unrelated.

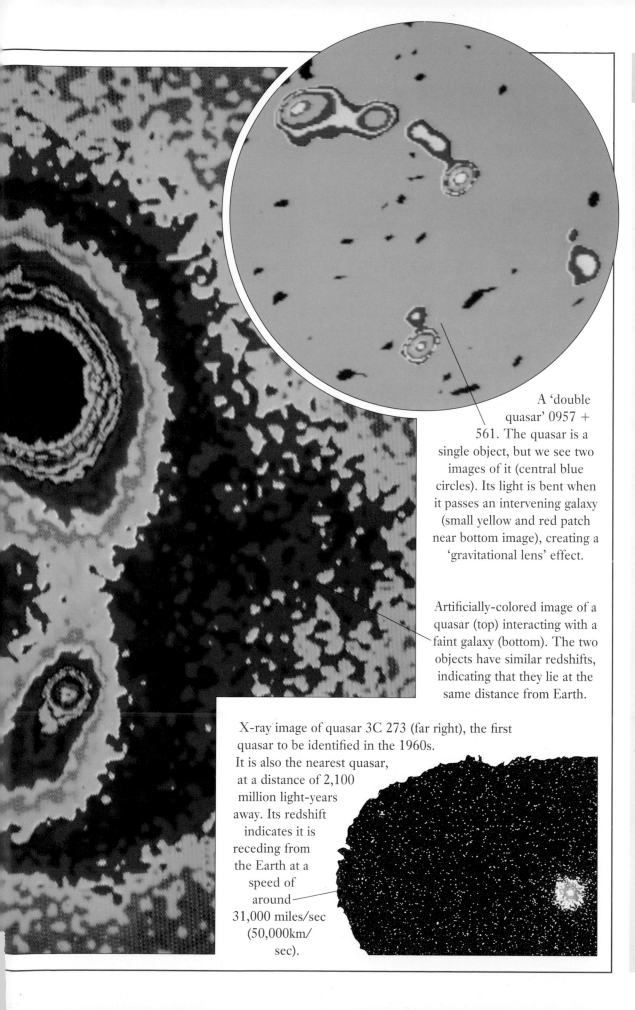

A 'double quasar' 0957 + 561. The quasar is a single object, but we see two images of it (central blue circles). Its light is bent when it passes an intervening galaxy (small yellow and red patch near bottom image), creating a 'gravitational lens' effect.

Artificially-colored image of a quasar (top) interacting with a faint galaxy (bottom). The two objects have similar redshifts, indicating that they lie at the same distance from Earth.

X-ray image of quasar 3C 273 (far right), the first quasar to be identified in the 1960s. It is also the nearest quasar, at a distance of 2,100 million light-years away. Its redshift indicates it is receding from the Earth at a speed of around 31,000 miles/sec (50,000km/sec).

❑ The most distant object so far observed is a quasar – a powerful radio source – 13,200 million light-years away. This object is moving away from us at a speed of over 94 percent of the speed of light.

❑ Quasars are amazingly bright objects. A quasar generates 100 times as much light as the whole of our Galaxy in a space not much larger than the Solar System.

❑ A massive black hole weighing billions of times more than the Sun would need to consume 10 Suns each year to keep a quasar fuelled and burning.

❑ In May 1983, a quasar was found that was emitting 1,000 million million times more energy than the Sun.

❑ Quasars, seen from the Earth, are only about as bright as a candle seen on the Moon. Astronomers need to amplify their light 10 million times to study quasars. If the energy from a quasar was collected by an Earth-bound radio telescope for 10,000 years, there would only be enough available to light a small bulb for a fraction of a second.

❑ The largest known structure in the Universe is a long band of quasars, 650 million light-years long and about 100 million light-years wide. The quasar band was discovered in 1991.

The biggest explosion of all time

Obviously, if the Universe is expanding now, then it must have been smaller in the past. We can deduce that, long ago, all the material in the Universe must have been squashed into a small ball of matter. This ball – called the cosmic egg – began to expand about 15,000 million years ago with the biggest explosion of all time, the Big Bang. The temperature of the early Universe was enormous. One hundredth of a second after the Big Bang, the Universe was the size of the Sun and the temperature was 180 million million °F (100 million million °C). Some subatomic particles – electrons, protons, neutrinos and neutrons – formed from the energy of the Universe. As time passed, the Universe expanded and its temperature dropped. After 100 seconds, the temperature had dropped to 1,800 million °F (1,000 million °C) – the temperature inside the hottest stars. Protons and neutrons came together to form helium nuclei. Later when the Universe was much older – some 300,000 years after the Big Bang – electrons combined with the nuclei to form hydrogen and helium atoms. The temperature was now a modest 5,400°F (3,000°C). After 500 million years, galaxies began to form from the hydrogen and helium gas. After 2,000 million years, the Milky Way was born. Then, 10,000 million years after the Big Bang, our Sun was formed.

Artist's impression of spiral galaxies being formed about 500 million years after the Big Bang, the titanic explosion which caused the Universe to come into being about 15,000 million years ago.

The spectrum of the cosmic microwave background radiation (red curve) obtained in 1990 by the Cosmic Background Explorer satellite. The spectrum confirmed the theory that the Universe started with a hot Big Bang.

Artist's impression of giant clouds of gas starting to condense into galaxies after the Big Bang. The theory of the Big Bang is based upon the fact that the Universe is still expanding, and on the discovery of radiation – the microwave background – that is believed to be the remnant from the explosion.

❏ The Universe is about 15,000 million years old. Put another way, if the years flashed by at the rate of one each second, the Universe would already be nearly 47 years old.

❏ It makes no sense to ask what the Universe was like before the Big Bang. Time, space, and the Universe, began with the Big Bang. There was no 'before.'

❏ Scientists estimate that 0.000,000,000,000,000,000, 000,000,000,000,000,001 seconds after the Big Bang, the Universe was the size of a pea, and the temperature had dropped to 18,000 million million million million °F (10,000 million million million million °C). One second after the Big Bang, the temperature was about 18,000 million °F (10,000 million °C).

❏ At the time of the Big Bang there was just one force, a 'superforce' that combined gravity, electric, magnetic, and nuclear forces into one. Later, as the Universe expanded, the superforce broke up and the distinct forces we recognize today came into being.

❏ The two lightest chemical elements, hydrogen and helium, were formed during the first 100 seconds of the history of the Universe from particles created in the Big Bang. Other elements are produced by nuclear reactions inside stars or in supernovae.

The end of everything

W ill the Universe expand forever? This depends upon how much material it contains. If there is enough material, the force of gravity will eventually slow down the expansion. Gravity acts like a 'glue' to hold the Universe together. Unfortunately, the amount of matter is difficult to measure because there is a great deal of material that we cannot see. This is called 'dark matter.' Until we know how much dark matter there is in the Universe, it is impossible to predict its ultimate fate. But, there are two possibilities. If there turns out to be relatively little dark matter, the Universe will expand forever. Eventually the Universe will be so large that the gas it contains will be spread thinly through vast spaces. No new stars will be born. The existing stars will one-by-one exhaust their nuclear fuel and die. The Universe will become a cold, dark immensity. On the other hand, if there is sufficient dark matter, the outward rush of the galaxies will eventually stop. The Universe may then start to collapse inward, with the galaxies falling toward each other. As the galaxies crowd together, the Universe would become hotter. The final stage would be a fireball like that which began the Big Bang – this is the Big Crunch. Perhaps, after the Big Crunch, the Universe will bounce back, and begin expanding again after a new Big Bang. Perhaps the history of the Universe will repeat in a series of Bangs and Crunches.

Collisions of subatomic particles in a particle accelerator mirror the conditions in the Big Crunch or Big Bang. Energy can materialize as particles, as shown in this image recorded at CERN, the European particle physics laboratory near Geneva.

Artificially-colored image of interacting galaxies, known as 'the mice.' They are located 270 million light-years away in the constellation of Coma Berenices. The long 'tails' consist of material drawn from their centers by gravity.

Radio contour map of galaxies M81 (bottom) and M92 (top) in collision. The contour lines show the distribution of radio-emitting hydrogen gas and a clear link between the two galaxies.

The concept of the Big Bang has led to theories which propose a series of parallel universes, perhaps in the form of a cluster of bubbles, such as we see in this artist's impression. Such parallel universes would be virtually undetectable, occurring perhaps in one or more extra dimensions.

❑ According to one theory, the Universe will end in the Big Crunch around 50,000 million years from now.

❑ Another theory supposes that the Universe will expand again after the Big Crunch in a new Big Bang. The cycle – Bang, Crunch, Bang, Crunch – will repeat every 65,000 million years. This is called the Oscillating Universe theory.

❑ Olbers' paradox is a simple question posed by German astronomer Heinrich Olbers in 1826: 'Why is the night sky dark?' If space was infinite and evenly filled with stars, then in whatever direction we looked we would see a star, and so the entire sky should be bright. There are several satisfactory answers to the paradox. One idea is that the Universe is not sufficiently old for light from very distant stars to reach us. The darkness of the night sky suggests that the Universe had a beginning.

❑ If the Universe expands forever, it might eventually become a single giant black hole. The monster black hole might form from smaller holes at the centers of the present galaxies.

❑ The laws of science are so accurate that, if current theories are correct, the future of the Universe can be predicted a million million million million million years ahead with more certainty than next month's weather.

STARFINDER

Northern Hemisphere Sky

Each hemisphere represents the northern and southern aspects of the sky as seen from northern latitudes. They show the brighter stars as they will appear at the noted local times on the months shown.

December 1, 23.30
January 1, 21.30
February 1, 19.30

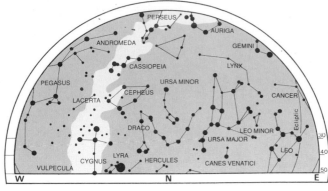

Looking South

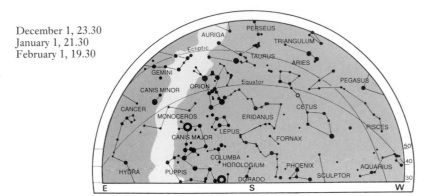

Looking North

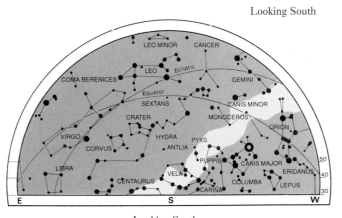

Looking South

March 1, 23.30
April 1, 21.30
May 1, 19.30

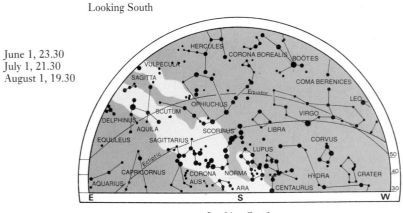

Looking North

June 1, 23.30
July 1, 21.30
August 1, 19.30

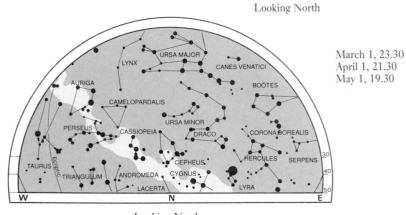

Looking South

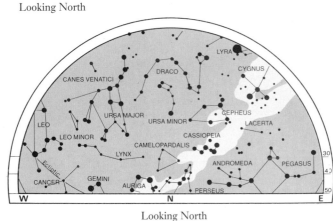

Looking North

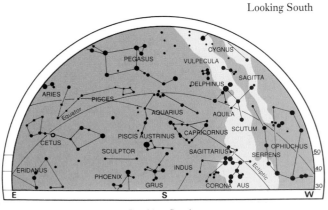

Looking South

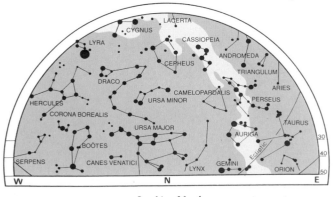

Looking North

September 1, 23.30
October 1, 21.30
November 1, 19.30

Southern Hemisphere Sky

Each hemisphere represents the northern and southern aspects of the sky as seen from southern latitudes. They show the brighter stars as they will appear at the noted local times on the months shown. The numbers in the border to the right of each hemisphere indicate the horizon for given degrees in latitude, so making the series useful for most highly populated regions.

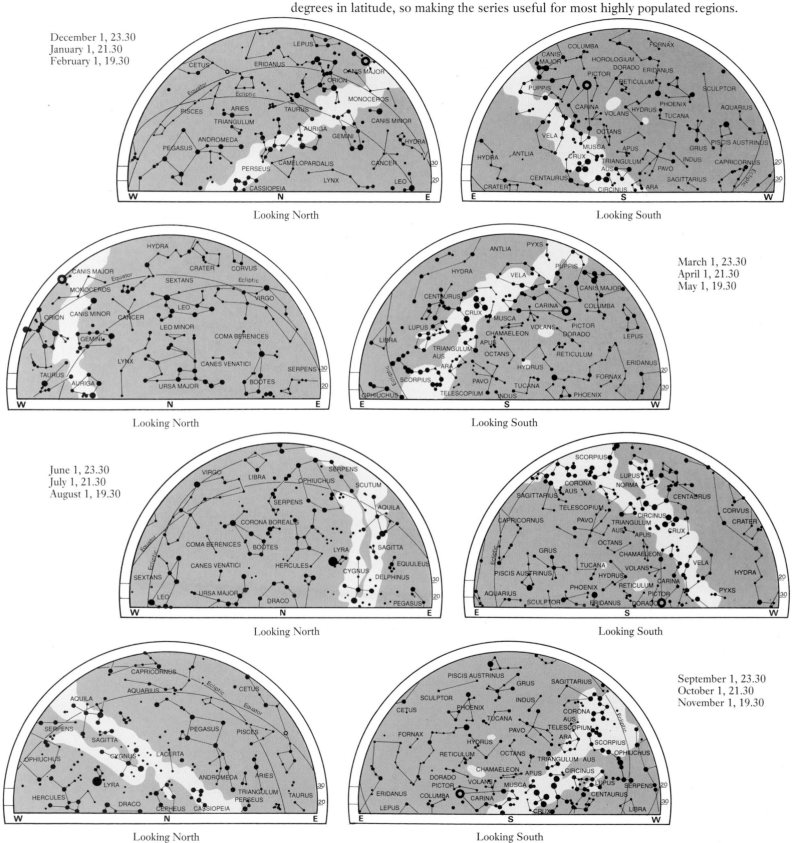

December 1, 23.30
January 1, 21.30
February 1, 19.30

Looking North

Looking South

Looking North

March 1, 23.30
April 1, 21.30
May 1, 19.30

Looking South

June 1, 23.30
July 1, 21.30
August 1, 19.30

Looking North

Looking South

Looking North

September 1, 23.30
October 1, 21.30
November 1, 19.30

Looking South

SUPERFACTS

Most common element ▶

The most common element in the Universe is hydrogen. The Universe contains about 10,000 atoms of hydrogen for every 1,000 atoms of helium and every 1 atom of other elements.

In the lap of the gods

All our companion planets in the Solar System are named after gods in Roman mythology, with the exception of Uranus, who was the Greek god of the sky. Planets orbiting closer to the Sun than Earth are called inferior planets; the others are superior planets.

The Leonids

During the night of November 16-17, 1966, a huge meteor shower passed over the mid-western U.S.A. At the peak of the shower 40 meteors per second (the equivalent of 144,000 per hour) were seen over Arizona, for a period of 20 minutes at 5 a.m. on November 17. The annual shower, which peaks every 33 years, is called the Leonids. The Leonid shower has been observed regularly since A.D. 902, with exceptional displays in 1002, 1101, 1202, 1366, 1533, 1602, 1698, 1799, 1833 and 1866. The Leonids are expected to produce another spectacular display on November 17, 1999.

Leaving home

In January 1990, Pioneer 10, the first spacecraft to leave the Solar System (an event that occurred on June 13, 1983 after 11 years of flight), was 4.4 billion miles (7.1 billion km) from the Sun and flying still deeper into space. Remarkably, it was still returning data to Earth. It is expected to continue traveling for another 2 million years.

The brightest stars

Name	Distance (light-years)	Luminosity (Sun=1)	Constellation
Sirius	8.8	24	Great Dog
Canopus	1,170	1,500	Ship Argo
Alpha Centauri	4.3	2	Centaur
Arcturus	36	100	Herdsman
Vega	26	50	Lyre
Capella	42	70	Charioteer
Rigel	900	60,000	Orion
Procyon	11	8	Little Dog
Achernar	120	360	River Eridanus
Betelgeuse	500	17,000	Orion
Hadar	420	8,600	Centaur
Altair	16	11	Eagle
Acrux	490	6,000	Southern Cross
Aldebaran	68	110	Bull
Antares	400	7,500	Scorpion
Spica	220	2,000	Virgin
Pollux	36	40	Twins
Fomalhaut	22	13	Southern Fish
Mimosa	425	5,200	Southern Cross
Deneb	1,600	70,000	Swan
Regulus	75	120	Lion

Note: The luminosity of a star is a measure of the total energy given out by the star.

The changing seasons

The planet Venus does not tilt on its axis as it goes around the Sun as other planets do, so it has no seasons. On Mars, the seasons are more exaggerated and last much longer than on Earth.

Close to home

Venus is the closest planet to Earth. It can come within 25 million miles (40 million km) of the Earth. Mars comes within 35 million miles (56 million km) of the Earth.

Speedy flyby

Voyager traveled under Saturn's ring system at a speed of 43,000mph (69,000km/h). At this speed the craft would take just six hours to reach the Moon from Earth and 90 days to reach the Sun.

Unpleasant place?

Hell is on the Moon. It is a crater 20 miles (32km) across and was named after a 19th century Hungarian astronomer, Maximilian Hell. It has nothing to do with the flaming inferno. Utopia, on the other hand, is a smooth, low-lying region on Mars.

The sting

Before the Yerkes Observatory in Chicago was opened, a carving depicting bees stinging a man was removed from a decorative panel near the main doors. It was felt that the millionaire who financed the observatory might think it was a joke at his expense, having being 'stung' for the money to build the observatory!

Boozy instrument

A piece of astronomical equipment is named after a famous beer. The instrument at the La Palma observatory, Canary Islands, was provided by the Danish brewing company Carlsberg, and is called the Carlsberg Transit Instrument.

Highest observatory

The world's highest observatory is at Boulder, Colorado. It is the Denver High Altitude Observatory, and is situated at an altitude of 14,097ft (4,296m), slightly higher than the observatory on Mauna Kea, Hawaii. Its main telescope has a mirror 24in (60cm) across.

Moon celebrities ▲

Moon craters and features are frequently named after famous people. The following people, among others, have craters named after them: Neil Armstrong, Tycho Brahe, Julius Caesar, Nicolaus Copernicus, Thomas Edison, Albert Einstein, Michael Faraday, Benjamin Franklin, Sigmund Freud, Vasco da Gama, Johannes Gutenberg, St. John, Johannes Kepler, Marco Polo, Isaac Newton, Plato, Jules Verne, Leonardo da Vinci, James Watt.

◄ Twinkle, twinkle, little star

The twinkling of stars is due to the Earth's atmosphere. A star is a steady point-like source of light but small air currents and atmospheric disturbances cause them to appear to vary in brightness. This explains why observatories are often constructed on the tops of mountains. The thinner air at altitude minimizes the distorting effects of the atmosphere.

Largest lens telescope

The world's largest lens telescope is at the Yerkes Observatory, Williams Bay, Wisconsin. It is 62ft (18m) long and has a lens 40in (101cm) across.

Not just ours

There are at least 60 moons in the Solar System. All the planets except Venus and Mercury have moons. The Earth has 1, Mars has 2, Jupiter has 16, Saturn has 21-23 (the uncertainty arises because of the difficulty of identifying the smallest moons), Uranus has 15; Neptune has 8, Pluto has 1. The moons range in size from Jupiter's Ganymede which is bigger than either of the two smallest planets (Pluto and Mercury), to tiny objects such as Mars' moon, Deimos, only 7 miles (12km) across.

Smallest constellation

The Southern Cross is the smallest consellation in the sky. It is only visible to observers in the Earth's southern hemisphere.

SUPERFACTS

Northern lights

The Northern lights (aurora borealis) are caused by huge eruptions on the Sun. These send out millions of small particles into space at speeds of about 1,000 miles a second (1,600km/s), and which reach the Earth in about 24 hours. They react with air particles in the upper atmosphere moving within the Earth's magnetic field releasing energy in the form of light. The equivalent display in the southern hemisphere is called the aurora australis.

The zodiac

The zodiac is the belt of the sky across which the Sun, Moon, and planets appear to us to move. The constellations or signs of the zodiac are Aries, Taurus, Gemini, Cancer, Leo, Virgo, Libra, Scorpio, Sagittarius, Capricornus, Aquarius, and Pisces, or in rhyme:

The Ram, the Bull, the Heavenly Twins,
And next the Crab, the Lion shines,
The Virgin and the Scales,
The Scorpion, Archer, and He-Goat,
The Man that bears the Watering Pot,
And Fish with glittering tails.

The speed of light

Light travels at a speed of 186,282 miles per second (299,792km/s). Light takes one-fiftieth of a second to travel from New York to London, 8 minutes to reach the Earth from the Sun, and 4.3 years to reach Earth from the nearest star, Proxima Centauri in the southern sky.

The light-year

1 light-year = 5.88 million million miles = 9.46 million million km. Another unit used to measure astronomical distances is known as the parsec (a contraction of the term, parallax second). 1 parsec = 3.26 light-years.

Big numbers ▲

If you count at the rate of one number each second, it would take 11½ days to count to 1 million, and 32 years to reach a billion (1,000 million). It is instructive to remember this when trying to grasp the scale of some of the enormous numbers that a study of astronomy involves.

The hottest star

In April 1992 the Hubble Space Telescope discovered the hottest star on record, 33 times hotter than the Sun. Burning at 360,000°F (200,000°C), the star lies at the heart of a nebula in the Large Magellanic Cloud.

GLOSSARY

Asteroid
A large chunk of rock that orbits the Sun, between Mars and Jupiter. There are many thousands of asteroids, measuring from less than 0.3 miles (0.5km) to 620 miles (1,000km) across.

Big Bang
The enormous explosion that occurred when the Universe came into being about 15,000 million years ago. Just after the Big Bang, the Universe was a small ball of extremely hot matter and radiation. The Universe then expanded and the stars, galaxies, and planets gradually formed.

Black hole
The region of space surrounding a very heavy and dense object whose gravity is so strong that not even rays of light can escape from it. Nothing falling into a black hole can ever get out again. Black holes are left over when very heavy stars explode.

Comet
A small body made of dust and gas that goes around the Sun in an oval-shaped path. If a comet comes near the Sun, the heat makes dust and gas form a long glowing tail.

Constellation
A group of stars that form a pattern or shape in the sky. Well-known constellations are Orion and the Great Bear (Ursa Major). There are 88 constellations covering the whole sky.

Eclipse
When one body in space blocks the light of another body in space. A solar eclipse occurs when the Moon temporarily blocks out the light of the Sun. A lunar eclipse occurs when the Moon passes into the shadow cast by the Earth.

Galaxy
A huge group of stars in outer space, containing millions of stars. The Sun belongs to a galaxy called the Milky Way. It is spiral shaped and contains about 100,000 million stars. Many galaxies are spiral shaped, but others have elliptical or irregular shapes.

Gravity
The force that draws any two bodies together due to their masses. The larger an object, the stronger is its force of gravity. The large mass of the Earth creates a strong gravitational force, so objects fall downward toward the Earth. The force of gravity between two bodies decreases as the bodies get further apart from one another.

Light-year
The distance light travels in one year, about 5.9 million million miles (9.5 million million km). Light-years are used by astronomers to measure the vast distances to the stars.

Meteoroid
A small piece of rock or dust traveling around the Sun. If a meteoroid hits the top layers of the Earth's atmosphere, it burns up and we see a 'shooting star.'

Meteorite
A large meteor that does not completely burn up as it falls through the Earth's atmosphere. It falls to Earth as a piece of stone or stony metal.

Milky Way
The faint band of light crossing the night sky, made up of innumerable faint stars; also the name given to our Galaxy.

Nebula
A cloud of gas and dust in space. Stars are born inside nebulae. The light given out by the young stars makes the gases in the nebula glow.

Neutrino
A tiny particle that can travel easily through solid material. Neutrinos are given out by the Sun, and by exploding stars.

Neutron star
A small star made up of neutrons which is formed when a large star explodes. Neutrons are particles found in the nuclei of most atoms. Neutron stars, also called pulsars, are left over after a giant star explodes.

Nova
A 'new star' or a star that suddenly shines more brightly for a short time and then fades. This happens when gas from one star flows to a nearby companion star and explodes as it hits the surface.

Nuclear fusion
The joining, or fusing, of the nuclei of two light atoms to make a heavier nucleus. This process releases large amounts of energy. Stars produce their energy by fusing hydrogen nuclei to make helium.

Planet
A large body that moves around the Sun. The planets of our Solar System are Mercury, Venus, Earth, Mars, Jupiter, Saturn, Uranus, Neptune, and Pluto.

Prominence
A huge flame that bursts from the surface of the Sun. The entire Earth could fit into one of these flames many times over.

Pulsar
A star that sends out regular bursts of radio waves or light. A pulsar is a spinning neutron star left over after a supernova.

Quasar
A small, very distant object that sends out powerful radio waves. They are hundreds of times brighter than ordinary galaxies and thousands of millions of light-years away. It is thought that a giant black hole inside the quasar produces the huge energy output.

Red giant
A large, red star, at least ten times the diameter of the Sun. Stars like the Sun swell up into red giants when they grow very old.

Redshift
The color change found in light from the distant galaxies which are moving away from us at great speed. Their light waves are stretched out by their motion and appear redder than normal.

Supernova
A very large explosion that occurs when a large star runs out of energy. It explodes, throwing off its outer layers and giving off as much light as thousands of millions of ordinary stars. After the explosion, either a neutron star or a black hole is left.

White dwarf
A small, dense star produced at the end of the life of a star like the Sun, when it has run out of fuel. A white dwarf the size of the Earth would weigh as much as the Sun.

INDEX

Page numbers in **bold** indicate major references including accompanying photographs. Page numbers in *italics* indicate captions to illustrations. Other entries are in normal type.

Voyage to discovery: the
Magellan probe is launched to
Venus from Shuttle *Atlantis.*

PICTURE CREDITS

The publishers wish to thank the following photographers and agencies
who have supplied photographs for this book. The photographs have
been credited by page number and position on the page: (B) Bottom,
(T) Top, (C) Center, (BL) Bottom Left, etc.

American Museum of Natural History:
Dept. of Library Services: 33(B), 55(T)

The Bettmann Archive: 11(CR)

Boeing Aerospace: 56-57

Hughes Aircraft Company: 35(C)

Frank Lane Picture Agency:
Ronald Thompson: 10(BR)

NASA: 25(B), 28-29, 29(T), 29(B), 30-31(T),
30-31(B), 34-35, 35(B), 39(T), 39(C),
39(BL), 41(C), 41(BR), 42(BL), 43(B),
44(B), 45(C), 46-47(B), 52(B), 107

Science Photo Library:
Ronald J. Allen and S. Sukumar: 84(B)
Julian Baum: 35(T), 41(T), 48-49, 50(B),
52-53, 68-69, 79, 97(B), 99(B), 103(T)
Sally Bensusen: 78(CR)
Brookhaven National Laboratory: 25(T)
Dr. Jeremy Burgess: 15(BL), 18(T), 26(T),
52(T), 59(B)
J.-L. Charmet: 13(BL), 16(T), 16(C), 16(B)
Dr. Kris Davidson: 74(BL)
Dennis di Cicco: 102
Ducros/Jerrican: 26-27
Dr. Martin England: 83(T)
Dr. Hilmar W. Duerbeck: 72-73
Fred Espenak: 16-17, 32-33, 62(C), 70(BL),
76(B), 80(B), 80-81, 84(CL)
Dr. Eric Feigelson: 83(B)
George Fowler: Front endpaper
GECO UK: 59(T)
Dr. Stephen T. Gottesman and Dr. L.
Weliackew: 98(B)

David A. Hardy: 37(T), 46(BR), 46-47(T),
49(T), 57, 66-67, 70(BR), 75(T), 78(BR)
Dr. William Hsin-Min Ku: 15(CR)
Arthur Johnson/U.S. Library of Congress:
30(BL)
Doug Johnson: 23(T)
Kapteyn Laboratorium: 88(TR)
Mehau Kulyk: 96(B)
Dr. Michael Ledlow: 36
Francis Leroy, Biocosmos: 78(BL)
Dr. Jean Lorre: 11(TR), 82-83, 84(CR),
90-91, 93, 104
Los Alamos National Laboratory: 66(C)
Rafael Macia: 61(BL)
Dr. Ronald J. Maddalena: 15(BR)
Magrath Photography: 37(CR)
Jerry Mason: 31(TR)
Max-Planck-Institut für Aeronomie/David
Parker: 53(B)
Max-Planck-Institut für Physik und
Astrophysik: 86(BL), 86-87
Dr. K. Milne/David Parker: 74-75
Hank Morgan: 96(T)
NASA: Title page, 15(T), 24(B), 24-25,
39(BR), 41(BL), 42(BR), 42-43, 43(T),
44-45, 45(T), 46(BL), 47(CR), 50(T),
52(C), 54, 56(BL), 56(BR), 64-65, 65(L),
76-77, 87(B), 89(TR), 95(B), back endpaper
NASA/Mehau Kulyk: 36-37
NOAO: Half-title page, 50-51, 62-63, 75(B),
81(T), 81(B), 82(T), 88-89, 89(TC), 90(T),
90(C), 92(B), 94, 94-95, 98-99
NRAO/AUI: 74(T), 82(B), 90(BL), 92(TR)
Claude Nuridsany and Marie Perennou:
19(T)
David Parker: 20(T), 22-23, 23(C), 86(CR),
98(T)
Mark Paternostro: 32, 54-55

Marion Patterson: 10(BL)
Ludek Pesek: 96-97
Roger Ressmeyer, Starlight: 20(B), 21(B),
23(B), 48, 87(C)
Dr. David Roberts: 95(T)
Dr. Ian Robson: 22(T)
Royal Greenwich Observatory: 18(B), 77(T),
91(T)
Rev. Ronald Royer: 51(CR), 58-59, 62(BL),
63(B), 78(T)
John Sanford: 17(T), 55(C), 60-61, 61(BR),
67(T), 103(B)
John Sanford and David Parker: 13(CR),
81(CR)
Robin Scagell: 10-11, 69(B), 71(B), 76(T)
Jerry Schad: 12-13, 13(TR)
David Scharf: 21(T)
Dr. Rudolph Schild: 64(TR)
Dr. Seth Shostak: 65(CR), 73
Smithsonian Astrophysical Observatory: 72(B)
Smithsonian Institution: 84(T)
Prof. Yoshiaki Sofue: 64(TL)
SPL: 8, 19(C), 63(T), 71(C), 92(TL)
Starlink/Rutherford Appleton Laboratory: 77(B)
Ian Steele and Ian Hutcheon: 55(B)
Sheila Terry: 26(B)
Alexander Tsiaras: 14
U.S. Geological Survey: 40-41
U.S.G.S./NASA: 38-39
U.S. Naval Observatory: 14-15
U.S. Navy: 66(T)
Nick Wall: 56(CR)
Tony Ward, Tetbury: 85

Starland Picture Library:
European Southern Observatory: 60(B)
National Optical Astronomy Observatories:
69(T), 69(C)

Jupiter's turbulent cloud formations as photographed by Voyager 1 in March 1979.